DAVID BRODY

Labor in Crisis

THE STEEL STRIKE OF 1919

with a new Bibliographical Afterword

University of Illinois Press
Urbana and Chicago

Illini Books edition, 1987
Published by agreement with Harper & Row, Publishers, Inc.
Copyright © 1965 by David Brody
Manufactured in the United States of America
P 5 4 3 2 1

This book is printed on acid-free paper.

Library of Congress Cataloging-in-Publication Data

Brody, David, 1930–
    Labor in crisis.

    Reprint. Originally published: 1st ed. Philadelphia :
Lippincott, 1965. (Critical periods of history)
    Bibliography: p.
    Includes index.
    1. Steel Strike, United States, 1919–1920.   2. Trade-
unions—Iron and steel workers—United States—History.
I. Title.   II. Series: Critical periods of history.
HD5325.I51919.B7   1987   331.89′269142′0973   86-30880
ISBN 0-252-01373-5 (alk. paper)

For
Sara Beth
and
Pamela

Contents

Preface

UNTIL RECENT TIMES, American labor history was a record chiefly of industrial war. Periodically the struggle burst into the open; mostly, it remained hidden and silent. But war it was. For men were contending for power. Should the terms of employment be fixed unilaterally by employers, or through collective bargaining with trade unions?

Employers resisted labor organization relentlessly and, for the most part, successfully. They penned the trade unions into a narrow field: the railroads, the coal mines, construction, clothing, certain skilled occupations. Early in the twentieth century, union membership leveled off at a mere one-tenth of the nonagricultural work force. Labor's signal failure occurred in the mass-production sector of the economy: motors, rubber, electrical equipment, food processing, and, above all, steel. Here, at the core of American industry, a massive open shop withstood the encroachment of organized labor.

Midway through the Great Depression, the balance swung to labor's side. By 1945, the labor movement counted fifteen million members; and powerful unions engaged in collective bargaining with major industrial companies. The stage of employer rule had finally passed.

This achievement was accompanied by other notable changes. Historically, voluntarism had ruled American labor relations. Unionization, no less than the determination of wages, hours and conditions, had fallen within the private sphere. But the Wagner Act of 1935—the key labor measure of the New Deal—canceled the employer's right to fight the organizing process and to refuse to bargain collectively. Governmental intervention thereby crucially assisted the union cause, but it also undermined the voluntaristic framework of American labor relations. A second change, of lesser ultimate importance, occurred within the house of labor itself. Before it could respond to the opportunity of unionizing the mass-production industries, the labor movement had to split apart. The emergence of the CIO shattered the settled structure and policies of American unions.

Why was unionization so long delayed? Why, when it finally came, did it require so sharp a break with the past? The answers must be pursued farther back in American labor history.

At one critical point, two decades earlier, unionization of the mass-production industries might have proceeded from the established labor-relations system. After World War I, trade unionism surged forward. Membership doubled; organization expanded into meat packing, textiles, motors, and other open-shop fields. The key was steel. If unionism entrenched itself here, the entire mass-production sector could be swept into the labor fold. A steel drive, launched in August 1918, gathered force in the postwar months. By the summer of 1919 more than 100,000 steelworkers had joined up. In September the steel movement struck the industry and, despite the heroic scale of the conflict, expired. From that defeat there would be no reprieve until new forces were unleashed by the Great Depression.

This book explores the events that culminated in the memorable steel strike of 1919. It assesses the roles of management, the trade unions, the industrial workers, the government, and the public. It seeks to explain why unionization failed before the New Deal era. And, by extension, it may illuminate a larger puzzle: why did mass-production unionism succeed when it did? The examination of a movement that failed has its historical uses.

When an invitation came to contribute a book on the steel strike of 1919 for this series, the proposal attracted me for several reasons. I had already written about the strike in an earlier volume, *Steelworkers in America: The Nonunion Era,* but my focus had changed since the publication of that book in 1960. Another set of questions, outlined above, could be asked of the events of 1918–19. Second, I wanted to look into such fresh sources as the George W. Perkins Papers and the manuscript records in the National Archives. Few things tempt an historian more than the chance to apply new materials to a familiar subject. I have depended on my earlier work for background purposes. But this book breaks new ground in its line of analysis and, as the documentation will reveal, in much of its information.

A number of debts need to be recorded here. Mr. Joseph D. Howerton of the National Archives indefatigably tracked down materials for me in the Social-Economic Section of the Archives. A former student, Miss Jan Conway, contributed her time and talents to finding important letters in the Woodrow Wilson and Joseph Tumulty papers in the Library of Congress. Professors Robert D. Cross and John A. Garraty read the manuscript critically, to my great benefit. A grant from the Council for Research in the Social Sciences of Columbia University permitted me to devote the summer of 1964 to completing a draft of the manuscript.

D. B.

1

Men of Steel

AT THE TURN of the twentieth century, "practical" men still dominated the management of the American steel industry. Trained in the business and charged with actual operations, these steelmakers were conditioned by the highly competitive era that had reached its climax in the depressed market of the mid-1890's. The industry, a steelman remarked, was then "a merciless game. . . . The profits were for those who pursued business relentlessly." Competitive pressures forced the full utilization of technological prospects, and the industry rapidly perfected the mechanized, continuous production of basic steel. "To stand on the floor of such a mill," an awestruck English visitor wrote, "and to witness the conversion, in the space of half an hour, of a red-hot steel ingot weighing several tons into finished steel rails 90 feet long . . . practically by the agency of unseen hands, is to gain new ideas of the possibilities of mechanism . . . evolved from the mind of the twentieth century American engineer." Steel manufacture was the ultimate demonstration "of the subservience of matter to mind."[1] The competitive and innovating stresses produced the distinguishing quality of American steelmen: the economizing temper.

The embodiment of this spirit was Andrew Carnegie. "Carnegie never wanted to know the profits," a partner noted. "He always wanted to know the cost." His firm,

---

* Superior figures refer to Notes at end of text.

the hardest competitor and the leading innovator in the industry, strove ceaselessly for economy of operations. "You are expected always to get it ten cents cheaper the next year or the next month," a former Carnegie manager explained. "The pressure is always on to make all the economies that you can." Department reports repeatedly claimed "the lowest cost yet obtained." The reward came in the climactic price war of 1897. Carnegie was marketing rails profitably at $14, a price below the production cost of his competitors. Carnegie's company earned $7 million in a year when the rest of the industry operated at a loss. He had the ability, a major competitor later admitted, to drive the entire industry to the wall.[2] A rising market prevented that. But the lesson had been driven home: economy measured excellence in steelmaking.

When Carnegie retired in 1901, he left behind him a cadre of junior partners and managers schooled in his ruthless spirit, his insistence on exact information and on rational calculation of alternatives, and his methods of exploiting subordinates. Most notable of these was Charles M. Schwab. Like others of Carnegie's "Young Geniuses," Schwab had been plucked from the laboring ranks, handed heavy responsibility and the incentive of a possible partnership. His rise was meteoric. President of the Carnegie Steel Company by thirty-five, he moved from there to operating head of the new United States Steel Corporation. Stymied by 1903, he left to assume control of the Bethlehem Steel Company. In a decade he built that moribund firm into a highly profitable enterprise, second only to U. S. Steel in size. Schwab applied to the task all of Carnegie's methods and—what Carnegie himself had lacked—an expert knowledge of steelmaking. A brilliant and captivating man, a lover of the good life, he demonstrated the continuing efficacy of the hard ways of the competitive era in a time when moderating forces were at work in the industry. Schwab was the idol and voice of the practical steelmen.

The spirit of economy determined the industry's labor policy. Steel men saw labor as an item of cost that, like any other, had to be narrowed to the irreducible minimum. This was, indeed, the main effect of technological innovation. Mechanized handling of materials, integration of the smelting, refining and rolling stages, and continuous rolling techniques all multiplied labor productivity by eliminating men or increasing operational speed. Steelmakers sought to increase productivity further through close supervision and rational disposition of work and scheduling. Theirs was essentially the outlook of scientific management (although not necessarily the actual prescriptions of the movement's founder, Frederick W. Taylor).

The other variable of labor cost was the wage rate. Long hours—in 1910, 30 per cent of the labor force worked a seven-day week; nearly 75 per cent a twelve-hour day—permitted the industry to hold down its hourly rates. And mechanization eliminated much of the high-paid work. But wage rates responded also to shifts in labor supply and demand, and were therefore less susceptible to control than the handling of labor. Complex although it was, wage determination had one sure rule: the denial of productivity as a guide. By divorcing wage rates from productivity, steelmen assured themselves a full return on economizing measures. Between 1890 and 1910, the labor component of total steelmaking costs shrank from 22½ to 16½ per cent.

Such achievement, steelmen felt, demanded unhindered and undivided decision-making by management. One U. S. Steel director, Percival Roberts, tried to explain to a Congressional committee the reasons for the twelve-hour day. "Who shall say [what] is the proper limit? . . . In the economies of this world, how shall we determine what that limit may be?" And the answer: "The laws of nature."[3] Given the objective of minimum labor cost, hours constituted a scientific question to be decided by objective criteria. That logic, of course, left no room for collective bargaining. Steelmaking generated a profound animus against trade unionism.

Nothing could divert it. The craft union in the industry, the Amalgamated Association of Iron and Steel Workers of North America, a power in the wrought-iron trade for many years, tried to accommodate itself to technological change in the emerging steel industry. Despite adverse effects on its membership, it bowed to innovation. The union discarded, in steel, output restriction and a variety of other protective practices that had evolved for the manual operations and fixed technology of wrought-iron manufacture. This was not—could not be—enough. Bilateral determination of the labor-cost factor, however reasonable the union was (and the Amalgamated Association was far from being invariably reasonable), ultimately had to be eliminated from steelmaking.

Wage determination revealed the heart of the matter. Skilled men under union contract worked on a tonnage basis, an arrangement deriving from the time of manual operations. Mechanization increased output per man-hour and raised the vital question: how should tonnage rates be adjusted? The best solution, from the steelmen's viewpoint, was to place a ceiling on take-home pay—that is, cut rates as productivity rose so income remained constant—and then, since machinery reduced skill levels, begin to cut into income also. The Amalgamated, while always admitting the justice of rate reductions when machinery increased output, claimed a share of the benefits for its membership. "There should be an end somewhere to labor standing the brunt of cheapened production," a union spokesman insisted.[4]

Work rules became equally troublesome. Even after dropping many of the practices drawn from the iron mills, the union retained a body of rules to protect the steelworkers on the job. Nearly sixty pages of "footnotes" in the union contract regulated the work process at the great Homestead plant. The Carnegie mills, said operating chief Henry C. Frick, failed "to turn out the product they should, owing to being held back by the Amalgamated men." Rid of union restriction, Frick would be free to maximize labor utilization, "selecting the best men and reorganizing the entire works, so that we shall not employ any more men than actually necessary." The economizing drive, as it sharpened, made trade unionism seem an insupportable brake on the steelmakers. Thus the chilling conclusion of a Carnegie partner: "The Amalgamated placed a tax on improvements, therefore the Amalgamated had to go."[5]

But did the industry have the power to drive out the union? Samuel Gompers, the founder of the AFL, judged the Amalgamated to be the strongest trade union in America at the end of the 1880's. Entrenched in wrought iron and expanding in steel, the union had a membership of more than 24,000 in 1891—about two thirds of the skilled men eligible to hold a union card. Employers—Andrew Carnegie included—treated the Amalgamated with cautious deference. Yet the very changes that were turning the steelmakers against trade unionism would enable them to defeat it. Mechanization undermined the manual skills constituting the vital source of craft-union power. And as steel firms grew in size and resources, their fighting capacity increased.

The issue came to a head in the decisive Homestead

strike of 1892. In contract negotiations that spring, the Carnegie company, intent on ousting the Amalgamated from the Homestead Works, deliberately provoked a strike. Carnegie and Frick were confident of their ability to destroy the union in a fight. Their funds were enormous, and the company's Braddock and Duquesne plants were nonunion and would maintain production no matter how long the Homestead mill was down. To cap it all, they doubted that the union could prevent the resumption of operations in the struck plant. By 1892, mechanization had so simplified steelmaking that untrained men could successfully replace the strikers. That key fact, evident to both sides, determined the course of the Homestead strike. Frick prepared to bring in strikebreakers; the steelworkers armed to keep them out. The result was a bloody gun battle between strikers and Pinkertons on July 6, 1892. Only disaster could issue from the bloody union victory. Troops arrived, the mill was reopened, and the strike collapsed. From these events came a solemn pledge: the Carnegie Steel Company "will never again recognize the Amalgamated Association or any other labor organization."[6]

The entire industry soon followed this example. One by one the big steel plants dislodged the Amalgamated until in 1903 the last was lost. The antiunion animus became fixed among the men responsible for operation and production. To these practical steelmakers, labor organization seemed incompatible with lower costs, and therefore needed to be relentlessly resisted.

The economizers, however, were no longer the only voices in the management of the industry. New leaders emerged who were not singlemindedly occupied with economy and who consequently saw trade unionism from another, less hostile perspective.

The competitive era reached a climax in 1900. To avoid a war between Carnegie and the rest of the industry, J. P. Morgan organized the United States Steel Corporation. This immense holding company controlled 60 per cent of the basic steel industry, including the Carnegie, Morgan and Moore properties, and nearly the entire capacity of the finishing lines. The merger made Morgan the dominant figure in the industry. His aim, a subordinate said, was nothing less than "to establish a community of ownership or a unified control over great industries as the only available means of restraining destructive competition."[7] But that task required not merely uniting the warring firms but also overseeing the pacified industry. J. P. Morgan and Company announced to investors that it would itself determine the "Plan of Organization and Management" of the steel corporation. The house of Morgan put its own partners on the board of directors, appointed much of the top management, and passed on the remainder. The imperious Morgan reserved for himself ultimate, if distant, authority.

His man in steel was Judge Elbert H. Gary. A man of handsome, gray dignity, Judge Gary was the very model of the senior corporation lawyer. He seemed, an admirer wrote, "A statesman rather than a man of affairs, an impression heightened by his deliberate speech and his appreciation of the finer meanings of words." J. P. Morgan's daughter Ann, in fact, found him altogether "too plausible." Judge Gary was a moralist, a Methodist, and a teetotaler. His was the credo of the golden rule in business: "We cannot make anything for our individual selves by injuring any other person, and we cannot assist . . . competitors in business without at the same time benefiting and assisting ourselves." H. L. Mencken once called him "the Christian hired man."[8] But in steel no one was laughing. For Judge Gary also proved to be iron-willed, fully the match for the gay ruthlessness of Charles Schwab.

From his post as chairman of the Executive Committee, Gary worked to implement Morgan's concept of "fair competition." Supported by his colleague in the steel corporation, Morgan partner George W. Perkins, Judge Gary set about discouraging cutthroat competition and stabilizing the market. "Nothing would be more helpful to the commerce of the entire country than to gradually reach a point where all articles we manufacture would have a price that was at least approximately stable," Perkins lectured the U. S. Steel operating head in 1909, "and we are certainly in a strong enough position now to make a vigorous effort to bring such a condition about in this period of prosperity. I believe the country generally expects us to make A-No. 1 goods, and to make them at reasonable prices." The subsidiary companies needed to be restrained from acting as if "our function is to get the very last dollar they can for certain articles when trade conditions make it possible."

This concern for the public interest sprang partly from selfish motives, for U. S. Steel was vulnerable under the Sherman Anti-Trust Act. The company's best defense, Judge Gary concluded, was the confidence of the public and the Government. "I am sure that we have anticipated a great many questions and situations that might have been unpleasant," Perkins wrote to Morgan in 1906, "and that the corporation is looked upon in Washington with more favor than perhaps any other one concern; and so far as the public is concerned . . . we are in a much better condition than almost any other concern." But Perkins hastened to add, "While our hopes are pretty buoyant as to how we will come out, we are alive to the fact that no one can tell what moment may bring about an unpleasant condition of things with us." So it was necessary to cultivate public opinion and to square corporation policy with considerations entirely beyond the ken of the operating men. That last fact constantly troubled the financial men. "I sometimes think that our subsidiary people do not appreciate that . . . the New York office is held responsible by the press and public for most everything that takes place," Perkins wrote in a blistering memorandum on the occasion of one lapse in Pittsburgh, "and that therefore the New York office should be consulted freely . . . in all matters that are of public interest."[9]

Judge Gary gradually made his way against the practical steelmen schooled in the competitive era of Andrew Carnegie. Backed by Morgan and other financial men attached to the corporation, Gary ousted Schwab and then another former Carnegie partner, William E. Corey, from the presidency, subordinated the rebellious subsidiary presidents, and consolidated his own position as real boss of U. S. Steel. Though he was never able entirely to prevent sharp practices, Gary nevertheless clearly directed the policies of the steel corporation after a decade in office.

Persuading the rest of the industry to accept co-operation proved unexpectedly difficult. Bethlehem, Republic, Jones and Laughlin, Youngstown Sheet and Tube, and other independent steel companies had toughened their competitive positions in the prosperous early years of the century. When hard times followed the financial panic of 1907, they began to slash prices in the fight for business. U. S. Steel leaders urged restraint. "After a long evening session last night," Perkins reported to Morgan in May 1908, "all the independent steelmen in the country joined our forces in feeling that prices should be maintained. . . . This time Judge Gary and I really had more trouble within our own ranks than with outsiders." The line could not be held, and in early 1909 U. S. Steel met the competition and cut prices. From the renewal of an unrestrained market grew the famous Gary dinners of 1909 and an understanding among the steelmakers for the future maintenance of prices. At a dinner in October 1909 Charles Schwab made the formal recantation of the competitive generation of steelmen, and Judge Gary intoned the phrases of "fair" competition—"fairness and friendship in business, cordial intercourse, confidence in each other, frankness in disclosure when information is properly requested."[10] The era of co-operation had arrived in the steel trade.

Large implications followed for labor policy. The financial men had their own views on the improvement of labor relations. The moral and humane considerations that justified fair competition carried over, partly by analogy and partly for sound strategic reasons, into the labor sphere. There was, said the Morgan partner Robert Bacon, "a new order of things . . . new rules of the game . . . in other human relations." In the relentless warfare of the 1890's, Judge Gary remarked, wages were cut to the bone and "strikes among the men were frequent." Now labor relations could be placed on a happier basis. The goal was a "community of interest between proprietors and wage earners."[11]

The U. S. Steel profit-sharing plan, which went into effect in January 1903, embodied the aims of the financial men. Employees could subscribe for preferred stock, pay in small installments while receiving dividends, and also get a bonus of five dollars a share for five years. George Perkins, the chief author of the scheme, added a special twist derived from his experience as an insurance magnate: bonuses which were not paid out (because the men sold their stock, left the employ of the corporation, or were deemed unworthy) would accumulate and be divided among the remaining stockholders after the five-year period. The profit-sharing plan seemed at the time a momentous innovation. From London, J. P. Morgan, Jr., congratulated Perkins on "the cleverness, wisdom and justice of the scheme. . . . It is a big step . . . towards mitigating the difficulties and dangers of the 'Capital versus Labor' question." Andrew Carnegie was carried away by his usual excess of enthusiasm: "This is to be the solution of the relations between Capital and Labor. If I were in manufacturing today, my ambition would be to have the first company in which every worker was my partner." Such was indeed the grand idea on which the plan vaguely rested. In 1915 Perkins asked Gary whether, since so many employees held stock, "it is not pretty nearly time . . . to put a man on the Board to represent them." They settled instead for inviting to the next stockholders' meeting some worker "who has done something . . . of signal importance to the Corporation's interest."[12] But the large intent, if not its realization, was clearly there.

In September 1914 Gary, Morgan, Henry Frick, and George Perkins—the big guns of U. S. Steel—met to discuss the stock subscription plan. The previous month employees had subscribed for over 40,000 shares, and the corporation was hard put to find so large a block. The market was inactive, and the stock stood at the high level of 109 or 110. Frick spoke up: he had 15,000 shares he was willing to sell "at a price." "We bantered him for a while on what he would take for it," Perkins recorded afterward. "We all tried our best to get him to sell at the market." Frick insisted on 115, arguing that any attempt to buy on the open market would push prices up to that point. The others bid 112, but Frick stuck to his price. Perkins was struck by the contrast between Frick, a former Carnegie partner and a product of the ruthless past, and himself and Gary, urging a generous disposal of the large block that would be distributed to thousands of workers "only buying one or two shares apiece." And Perkins reflected: "There could scarcely be a more striking illustration of the changing ownership in the steel business."[13]

The transfer of power manifested itself in other ways. In the spring of 1909 Gary and Perkins won a signal victory over the operating men on wage policy. As prices fell in an openly competitive market, the independents began to cut wages. U. S. Steel's financial men resisted the pressure of subordinates to follow suit. The question, Perkins reported in April to Morgan, "has given me a great deal of anxiety." The policy of wage stability was being maintained thus far, but "there is a great deal of opposition and we may not be able to carry it through to the end." Gary and Perkins, backed by Morgan, prevented a decision until business began to revive. On May 19, 1909, Perkins cabled Morgan jubilantly that the independents were rescinding the reductions.[14] Wage stability, the counterpart of price stability, thereafter became settled policy in the industry. Gradually, too, steel companies evolved a broad range of labor reforms: safety, accident insurance, pensions, plant sanitation, community improvement. The welfare programs, it is true, were spurred by Government investigations and public criticism of labor conditions in the industry. But the financial men, responsive though they were to public opinion, also sincerely desired to advance the workers' welfare. "The greater my experience in matters of this sort," Perkins explained to Cyrus H. McCormick of International Harvester, "the more convinced I am that the employees of a large concern, who are properly handled and fairly treated, are as fair and honorable with the management of their concern as anyone could wish them to be."[15] It seemed a far cry from earlier labor policies dictated by the iron logic of the cost books.

[24]

Might not the industry view of trade unionism also be liberalized? This seemed entirely possible at the outset. The financial men clearly lacked the operating men's deep animus against organized labor. Nor had their contact with trade unions, such as it was, been uncongenial. Morgan's activities in the 1890's had centered mainly on the railroads, which dealt amicably with the railroad brotherhoods. Gary had headed the Federal Steel Company, where good relations with the Amalgamated Association still existed when the company was merged into U. S. Steel. Shared interests brought the financial men together with labor leaders in the National Civic Federation and, occasionally, in political meetings. Perkins and Gary worked actively with Gompers, for instance, in an attempt to amend the Sherman Anti-Trust Act in 1908. When the anthracite strike of 1902 drew the Morgan interests into the immediate sphere of labor-management relations, Perkins backed Mark Hanna's activities on behalf of the strikers. "We cannot afford to do anything but support his efforts for a good many reasons," he wrote to Morgan. Perkins was, in fact, instrumental in ending the strike on terms favorable to the union.[16]

Conceivably, therefore, the industry's labor policy might have been reversed by the financial men. Responsible unions might help build the stable, co-operative labor relations envisaged by the new leaders of the steel industry. J. P. Morgan did indeed tell Amalgamated officers, during the strike against U. S. Steel in 1901, that he sympathized with organized labor and did not object to the eventual unionization of the entire steel corporation. That may have been an exaggeration to meet the immediate crisis. But clearly the financial men considered the union question an open one in the beginning. So the National Civic Federation was anxious "that every influence be brought to induce Mr. Morgan and his friends to 'start right.' "[17] The outcome proved otherwise.

The Amalgamated Association immediately bungled. It chose to strike while U. S. Steel was in its first, vulnerable months. The advantage was wasted by poor strike tactics and the failure to accept a favorable offer. The defeated Amalgamated, fatally weakened by the terms of settlement, now faced an immense corporation that was on its feet. The union had squandered most of its credit with the new industry leaders. It had provoked the conflict, then dishonored contracts, and finally enraged J. P. Morgan during settlement negotiations. (Morgan considered it a breach of faith that the union executive board turned down a proposed agreement between him and Amalgamated officers.) The regal banker, who was known to rest weighty decisions on slighter grounds than these, wrote off the Amalgamated Association. So the specific situation in U. S. Steel, involving an organization both weak and discredited, hardly encouraged union sympathies among the financial men.

Nor did their evolving experience in the steel industry. Trade unionism, the bankers soon realized, was incompatible with the underlying paternalism of their labor views. "We know what our duty is," Judge Gary said; "we know what the rights of our employees are, and we feel obligated . . . in keeping their wages up and in bettering their conditions and keeping them in a position where they enjoy life. We are the ones to lead in this movement." There was, he ultimately insisted, "no necessity for labor unions."[18]

The U. S. Steel leaders feared public criticism on the union issue. They refrained from exacting harsher terms from the Amalgamated in 1901 to avoid "the position of openly oppressing organized labor." When a strike broke out among Minnesota iron miners in 1907, Perkins assured

Morgan that steps were being taken "so that the public would understand the situation and that the newspapers would not get started off on the wrong track."[19] But now steelmen perceived a persuasive rationale for a tough stand against organized labor. The open-shop idea was spreading in these years of general reaction against unionism. The basic concept of shops open to union and nonunion men alike, and, as a corollary, free of union recognition and contract, was hardly new. Now, however, it was popularized and invested with powerful ideological overtones. The open shop became a defense of personal liberty and, as a U. S. Steel spokesman proclaimed, of "the principles upon which the government of this country was founded."[20] A hard line against unions became publicly defensible.

Before the end of the steel corporation's first decade, the financial leadership had completed its education. On June 1, 1909, the U. S. Steel sheet and tin-plate subsidiary announced "all its plants after June 20, 1909, will be operated as 'open' plants." It was the end of the road for collective bargaining in the steel industry. Although some union organization remained on the fringes, the mass-production industry had taken its stand as a bulwark of the open shop.

Steel was challenging the American labor movement in a most fundamental way. The unions' failure went beyond this one massive industry. The characteristics of steel manufacture—mechanizing technology, economizing practice, multiplant operation, oligopolistic structure—were shared by the entire mass-production sector of the economy emerging at the opening of the twentieth century. Having lost steel, where it had been entrenched, organized labor held little hope of breaching the automobile, rubber, oil-refining, food-processing, or other mass-production industries. The steel industry tested labor's ability to respond to the mass-production revolution. The cause of the Iron and Steel Workers, observed Samuel Gompers, was "the cause of labor."[21]

The failure of the Amalgamated Association revealed the inadequacy of the older ways of American craft unions. Formed in 1876 from a merger of the three craft organizations of puddlers, heaters and rollers, and roll hands, the union encompassed the iron- and steel-making skills. Although its formal jurisdiction gradually expanded —beginning in 1889, even laborers could be admitted "at the discretion of the Subordinate Lodge"—in reality the union remained an organization of skilled men. Only 800 of the 3,800 Homestead workers in 1892, for instance, belonged to the Amalgamated. Defeat at that point proved the bankruptcy of the union's exclusion policy in a modern steel mill. Mechanization deprived craft unionism of its main source of strength in the basic industry: the indispensability of the skilled men. Year by year the loss of remaining union mills corroborated this fact. Yet the Amalgamated held to its craft line for an inordinate—and fatally wasted—period.

Doomed as it was in basic steel, craft unionism still seemed viable in the finishing branches of the industry, and in the declining wrought-iron field. Sheet and tin-plate manufacture, which grew rapidly after 1890, depended on skilled manual labor. The union's success here coincided with its failure in basic steel, and enabled the cautious Amalgamated leaders to escape the need for a painful organizational adjustment. A prosperous, if restricted, future among skilled workers apparently awaited the Amalgamated. Its contracts in 1900 covered three quarters of the sheet mills and nearly all the tin mills in the country, and "Tin Workers" had been appended to its title.

The strike against U. S. Steel in 1901 cut short the confident expectations of the craft leaders. Technological advances, especially in sheet rolling, had lessened the skill requirements in sheet and tin mills, and a significant number of plants were able to resume operations with strikebreakers. The greater threat, however, resided in the immense economic power of new business concentrations. It was, indeed, the union's move to consolidate its position before that power could be brought to bear which caused the 1901 strike. The Amalgamated demanded contracts for *all* plants of the three U. S. Steel subsidiaries—American Tin Plate, American Sheet Steel, and American Steel Hoop —that still seemed susceptible to craft organization. Not only did the union fail to achieve its objective, but it lost its hold on fifteen mills that had been reopened by strikebreakers. While still recognized for its remaining mills, the Amalgamated was now truly at the mercy of the Steel Trust. The strike settlement included a remarkable clause prohibiting the Amalgamated from extending its organization within U. S. Steel. Thereafter, the union followed an unaggressive, conciliatory course, "giving way to every request" of the steel corporation. The Amalgamated in effect placed its fate in the hands of management. It was a notable lapse from a ruling maxim of American trade unionism: that labor progress depended on economic power.

Nor did the AFL see in the 1901 disaster the need for another approach to steel. The primary responsibility rested with the Amalgamated. And the union's actions during the strike obscured the real meaning of the conflict. Amalgamated President T. J. Shaffer displayed an astounding facility for alienating his natural allies. To cap his inepitude in the strike, he wildly accused Gompers and other labor leaders of treachery.[22] U. S. Steel, on the other hand, managed to seem reasonable and friendly even while cutting the heart out of trade unionism in its mills.

Gompers himself testified to his esteem for the steel corporation's leaders.

The open-shop announcement of 1909 dispelled the union's lingering illusion that there could be any substitute for effective organization. Shocked by the unexpected blow, the Amalgamated called its men out of U. S. Steel's sheet and tin mills. And the union vowed to organize the entire corporation. It had not acted earlier for fear of jeopardizing the existing contracts. "Now that restraint is off," asserted an Amalgamated official, "we do not propose to stop our work with the tin-plate department, but will press organization in every class of the mill." The challenge reverberated through the labor movement. "Never was a more unjust contention instituted than the onslaught of the steel trust on the Amalgamated Association," charged the AFL. Gompers promised "to help . . . to the very fullest of my opportunities and with whatever strength and ability I have." A flow of contributions permitted the Amalgamated to wage a stubborn fight against the steel corporation for fourteen months before capitulating. Thereafter, U. S. Steel was marked "as the most formidable and aggressive enemy that the movement has to contend with," and the highest priority was given to "the thorough organization of all branches of its business."[23]

The commitment raised an issue of basic importance: the strategy of organization in mass-production industry. The best approach, it seemed clear even then, was industrial unionism—bringing all the workers in one industry into a single national union. This would guarantee unity of action and avert the manifold difficulties of artificially dividing a labor force made occupationally indivisible by mass-production techniques. Industrial unionism, however, was stymied by the existing structure and rules of organized labor. The craft unions, who stood to lose by industrial unionism, dominated both the conventions and the inner counsels of the AFL. The desire to attack the mass-production fields, real as it was, had to be limited by considerations of constitutional rule, vested interest, and subtle power realities. As the definitive Scranton Declaration of 1901 had said, the AFL would adhere as closely to the "fundamental principle" of organization "on trade lines . . . as the recent great changes in methods of production and employment make possible."[24]

Its complacency shattered by the open-shop declaration, the Amalgamated Association publicly repudiated the policy of limiting membership to skilled workers, and dispatched organizers into nonunion territory. Circulars urged all steelworkers to "join [the] . . . fight for the emancipation of yourself and fellow workmen from the industrial tyranny of the steel masters of the country." "There is but one way to relieve [the] situation for the men in the iron and steel industries," an Amalgamated leader proclaimed. "That is to organize them into a powerful organization, embracing all the branches of the steel and iron industry, beginning with the blast furnaces." At its convention of 1910, the union took the necessary formal steps. The constitution was changed to eliminate skill as a basis for membership, and the initiation fee of $5 was reduced to $2.50 for unskilled steelworkers—an important dispensation for the low-paid men. The Amalgamated thus did voluntarily what the AFL could not force it to do: it made a place for the mass-production workers in steel.

The Federation encouraged this transformation up to a point. Unlike many others, Gompers had long recognized that organizational strength in steel required the inclusion of the unskilled. As far back as 1899, he had so argued with the reluctant secretary of the Amalgamated Association. Gompers's view now gained wider support within the labor movement. A special AFL conference in December

1909 favored a steel union to "which all workers in the iron, steel and tin-plate industry would be eligible." But past policy also dictated jurisdictional limits. In their first enthusiasm Amalgamated leaders had apparently envisaged a union that would "comprise every class of mechanic and laborer—in other words, an industrial organization." The AFL immediately made clear that an expanded Amalgamated could "not interfere with jurisdictions already recognized by the AFL."[25] Craft unions covering interindustry trades—machinists, carpenters, stationary engineers, and so on—surrendered none of their jurisdictional rights in the steel mills. What the Amalgamated had was a kind of residual jurisdiction over everyone not covered by one of the other unions. This was as close as the AFL could come to industrial unionism without violating its rules of trade autonomy and exclusive jurisdiction.

Mounting an organizing drive was the immediate assignment. The immense task far surpassed the means of the Amalgamated. At the AFL convention of November 1909, President P. J. McArdle asked the labor movement to mobilize its resources against the steel corporation. "The thorough organization of all branches of its business is the most important and necessary work that could engage the attention, time and effort of the AFL." Thirty-six unions consequently sent representatives to a conference in Pittsburgh on December 13, 1909. There a program was adopted: every national union to assign at least one organizer to a steel drive; the AFL to contribute part of its organizing staff and the central labor bodies in steel towns to do voluntary work; and funds to be raised through appeals issued by the AFL Executive Council. The joint campaign barely started; it ended within a month with no visible results. "I can't escape the conviction," wrote Gompers in disappointment, "that an opportunity which might have proven of most intense interest and advantage to the cause has been thrown away."[26]

Gompers had pleaded for organizers. "Can the American labor movement as represented by the AFL, afford to allow this undertaking to be a failure without an honest consistent effort being made? I think not. I hope not."[27] But, as tempers cooled, the national unions ignored Gompers's plea. Only a half dozen organizers were actually contributed, and not all of these came from the twenty or more unions with a jurisdictional interest in steel. The national unions were the power centers of the labor movement, and consequently they, rather than the Federation, received the bulk of the income. But only the Federation had the breadth of outlook required to cope with the challenge of mass production. It remained to be seen whether the national unions could be persuaded that, as Gompers said, theirs was "the responsibility for success or failure."

Another weakness was in the character of the Amalgamated. Fired into an uncharacteristically aggressive mood by the U. S. Steel attack, the union quickly fell back into its accustomed ways. From its small membership of well-fixed craft workers on the fringes of the industry came no impetus to organize the men on the blast furnaces and in the steelmaking plants. The series of union leaders—T. J. Shaffer, P. J. McArdle, John Williams, Michael F. Tighe—were conservative careerists, craft-conscious in outlook, anxious above all to preserve their stable, if tiny, union, reluctant to engage in the hard job of organizing steelworkers. The natural choice to head the steel drive started in December 1909, McArdle accepted the job unwillingly, quickly lost heart, and soon sent the organizers back to their home unions. Gompers found this out too late to reverse the decision.

Nor did the union reveal any means for its own regeneration. A minority element did demand, as one dissident wrote in 1912, that "the Amalgamated Association should at once become a militant progressive organization, a fighting force in the work of uniting the men in the iron and steel industry in this country into one big organization. We should place our organizers in the field among the nonunion men to work in conjunction with the AFL organizers."[28] But such sentiment spent itself in futile secessionist movements.

The Amalgamated was thoroughly unsuited to meet labor's needs in basic steel. Yet this unpromising organization in the backwash of the labor movement retained its central place in the future of unionism in steel. For, under the governing rules of the AFL, there was no way by which the Amalgamated could be pried from its steel jurisdiction or by which a more vigorous union could share the field legitimately. Sore in his disappointment over McArdle's defeatism in 1910, Gompers continued to regard his own efforts as "this fight for the Amalgamated Association."

The steelmakers' challenge was eliciting a response from organized labor. Clearly it was not the best possible. Yet there were grounds for hope. Labor was firmly committed to unionizing the steel industry, and also persuaded that mass production required a departure from past practice. Now the labor movement awaited the opportunity that would justify the effort to organize the steelworkers.

Unionization could succeed only when it was actively demanded by the laboring ranks. No such call came under the normal industrial conditions of the early twentieth century. Trade unionism drew little response from the steelworkers before World War I.

The industry itself raised formidable obstacles. Before 1900, steelmen had blatantly utilized yellow-dog contracts.

[34]

Even in 1910 one large independent required a signed statement from workmen denying union membership and pledging "not in any way, directly or indirectly, [to] join or have anything to do with any union of any kind whatever." For the most part, steel employers now claimed to run an open shop: "We do not ask whether they are union men or not." That may have been so in quiet times. But when organization grew, steelmen—of open-shop persuasion or otherwise—cracked down hard. "We know the policy under which a union man is done away with," a Bethlehem worker testified. "They don't do it openly but they punish a union man for many things a nonunion man can do freely. . . . I have seen good mechanics penalized that was as union men [*sic*]." Steelworkers were convinced, Government investigators concluded, "that any attempt on their part to extend or organize unions . . . would result in the discharge of the men responsible for such a movement. Furthermore . . . for any man to acknowledge his affiliation was likely to prejudice his interests if it did not result in his discharge." Fear, in fact, touched any act of personal assertion. A U. S. Steel employee appealed to the Secretary of Labor for the abolition of the twelve-hour day "as we dare not say anything about it or we [lose] our jobs."

Efficient methods kept workers in hand. "The men . . . do not relish being watched, but their steps are 'dogged' while they go about amidst smoke, dust and dirt, at the behest of a swearing and blasphemous 'Hurry-up regime.' . . . The men are under a Despotism. Discharge is followed by the dreaded and unjust BLACKLIST." When organization secured a foothold at the main Bethlehem plant in the spring of 1918, the company compiled a list of 91 activists under this title: "These Men Are Undesirable and Should Not Be Employed." At a meeting on May 20, 1918, a local leader testified, "we discovered a man taking notes of the proceedings. . . . He was a Pinkerton detective operating among the Bethlehem Steel Works employees." A careful contemporary investigator concluded that "all of the steel companies have effective methods of learning what is going on among the men."[29]

Company power extended beyond the mill gates. Homestead, South Chicago, Gary, and East Youngstown owed their existence to the steel works, and could be counted on to support the status quo. Local opposition to unionism became palpable at moments of labor strife. Denunciations rang from pulpits and newspapers; merchants and landlords refused to extend credit; public officials invoked ordinances and injunctions to prevent mass meetings, picketing and parades. When a newly formed union rented a hall in Bethlehem in April 1918, the police chief told the owner to return the deposit and keep the agitators off the property. He flatly refused a direct request to permit meetings. Nothing came of the union's appeal to the mayor: he was a company vice president.

The full force of community hostility struck union organizers who ventured into steel towns. Normally they were ordered away by the police. Sometimes they were jailed or mobbed. "It is unsafe to enter the town, as you are in danger of being attacked at any moment," reported an Amalgamated organizer after being driven out of Vandergrift, Pennsylvania. The burgess there justified his policy readily. His duty was to prevent any activity that "would mar the peace and harmony that pervades the entire community."[30] To the limits of his horizon, the steelworker saw a power structure hostile to trade unionism.

Other pressures, less ominous in character, also counteracted the union appeal. For the high-paid steelworkers, mechanization played the critical role. Before the technological revolution, steelworkers had felt keenly their personal independence and craft solidarity. Both qualities, which had made them superb union material, diminished as machinery undercut manual skills. In the modern steel mill, there were few jobs that could not be filled by someone on a lower rung of the employment ladder. Skill no longer conferred job security, experience no longer assured advancement. Competitiveness therefore intensified. Interviewers heard the recurrent phrase: "Each man is out for himself." The whims of the boss now outweighed the impersonal test of skill. The vital interests of the steelworkers—security and advancement—increasingly hinged on the good will of the employer.

Company policy encouraged dependency. Under the benevolent influence of Judge Gary, welfare programs assumed a larger part of the industry's labor policies. It became common to make available low-interest loans for the purchase of homes, or to offer company houses for rent on good terms. Workers benefited from improved housing, but they paid with a tighter attachment to the employer. Some men "would not think of" buying a house, one steelworker explained, "for the reason that in the event of anything coming between them and the mill there is not much chance of obtaining steady employment near where they live." Loyalty was the *quid pro quo* of a variety of other welfare schemes. Stock purchase plans and bonuses placed a premium on "long and faithful service." U. S. Steel's profit-sharing plan paid bonuses to participants who worked through the year for the company and, as evidenced by the reports of superiors, "showed a proper interest in its welfare and progress." When Charles Schwab came upon this phrase in the original proposal, he penciled in an objection: "I would omit this. It would enable the officials to nullify the plan."[31] But discretionary power was essential to the plan's concept. Automatic bonuses would be a right, not a reward. The plan's authors

[37]

wanted to give workers cause for fidelity and industry and, when this paid off in the voluntary bonus, reason for gratitude to the company.

Paternalism actually demanded a very high level of management performance. In the nature of things, the responsible executives rarely measured up to the task. On April 11, 1910, U. S. Steel officials met to consider a proposal for beneficial associations to be financed partly by the employees. The labor-relations men instantly opposed the idea. If the plan was voluntary, they argued, few would participate. If it was compulsory, on the other hand, it would "tend to decrease rather than increase the workman's disposition to help himself." Nor would the company receive credit. "It would be impossible to make the men understand that their payments constituted but a small proportion of the total amount furnished by the companies." Finally, the plan's concept was itself bad: "Injured men, although able to go to work, would claim disablement if they began to receive part wages immediately after the accident." Such mean-mindedness by the administrators of welfare work undermined its basic purpose: to attach workingmen to the company. As Judge Gary told his subsidiary presidents, the employees should be shown "that it is for their interests in every respect to be in your employ."[32] That demanded sensitivity to the psychological, no less than material needs of the steelworkers.

The industry's generosity, moreover, flowed in a narrow channel. Steel companies sought to fasten skilled men to the company, but the unskilled they considered a "floating labor supply." During slack periods, U. S. Steel often provided work for its "permanent" force by firing casual laborers. The low-paid men benefited relatively little from company housing, pensions, or stock-purchase plans. Nor were their earnings adequate even for a bare

subsistence. Skilled men lived well enough. On twenty
dollars a week, a Pittsburgh family in 1907 could afford
a six-room house, a varied diet, and the small comforts of
industrial life. The semiskilled steelworker lived closer to
the bone, but above the level of subsistence and minimal
working-class decency. To investigators, it seemed impossible for the mass of steel laborers, who earned under
two dollars a day, to live even at the subsistence level.
A family of five in Pittsburgh needed fifteen dollars a
week in 1910. No unskilled steelworker received that
much, and many earned under ten dollars a week. Working an 84-hour week, men still could not support their
families. Lacking both the company attachment and the
adequate compensation of the skilled men, the common
laborers nevertheless demonstrated neither a greater sense
of grievance nor more inclination toward trade unionism.

Most of these unskilled laborers were recent immigrants.
Flocking to this country in the first decade of the century,
the Poles, Croats, Serbs, Slovaks, Hungarians, and Italians
filled the bottom ranks of workers in the steel industry.
They constituted, for example, nearly two thirds of the
common labor in a typical large steel plant in 1910. Southern and Eastern Europeans, according to the U. S. Immigration Commission, made up 33.4 per cent of the total
labor force in iron and steel in 1907.

The recent immigrants differed profoundly from the
English-speaking men in the mills. Displaced peasants,
they regarded their jobs only as a means of accumulating
the money to purchase land or raise the mortgage in a
village in Austria-Hungary or the western provinces of
Imperial Russia. A dollar seventy-five a day was not low
by their standards, nor did they expect to live like Americans. Most immigrant steelworkers left their families
behind. The Immigration Commission discovered that
one third were unmarried, and that of the married men

who had been in the United States less than five years, three quarters had come alone. Those with families supplemented their incomes by lodging their countrymen. For a few dollars a month, a Polish steelworker could have a bed (which might have another occupant while he was at work) in the crowded rooms of the "boarding boss." At the end of each month the bill for food, purchased and cooked by the wife, was divided among the adult males in the household. The boarding-boss arrangement permitted a common laborer to put aside as much as half of his earnings.

Saving money was the one essential for the peasant steelworkers. Their jobs were exhausting and dangerous; their accident rate much exceeded that of English-speaking employees. Life in the Hunkyvilles of the steel towns was harsh and dismal, relieved only by the companionship of countrymen and the wild sprees on "pay night." But the hard existence in America would have an end: when the hoard of dollars rose high enough, the immigrant would go home. The ruling criterion therefore was not the wage rate, the kind of work, or the outlandish way of American life, but employment itself. "It is a golden land so long as there is work," a Polish worker wrote, "but when there is none, then it is worth nothing."[33]

The home village was the immigrant goal. Many did return to Eastern Europe: forty-four left for every hundred that arrived from 1908 through 1910. But most did not. Time and experience changed men. Distance loosened the binding ties of the village, weakened the inherited values of peasant life, and dimmed the memory of the past. Wives came, and the immigrants put down roots in the mill towns. The job was no longer a temporary expedient. This gradual change coincided with a real improvement in work prospects. Available statistics show this critical fact: the percentage of recent immigrants in skilled jobs and higher pay brackets moved upward in direct proportion to their length of time in this country. While remaining distinct on ethnic grounds, the Eastern Europeans otherwise merged with the native Americans, Britons, Irish, and Germans who dominated the skilled occupations in the steel mills.

Mobility shaped the immigrant adjustment to employment in steel. The recent arrivals expected to return to Europe with their precious savings: that seemed a fair exchange for whatever hardship the exile years exacted. These men either moved up into the skilled ranks or left discouraged during slack times, or—what was in reality least likely—left with money enough to fulfill their peasant purposes. The process did not permit a crystallization of grievances that could be exploited by organized labor. The steel industry, complained the AFL, employed men "who are unfamiliar with the moral and living standards of this country."

The mobility pattern contained one weak link. For the immigrant, the crucial necessity was that the work be uninterrupted. But the steel mills could not provide steady employment. The industry was highly susceptible to the business downturns that hit the economy at three- or four-year intervals after 1900. And company policy, which considered the unskilled to be casual labor, exaggerated the impact of recessions. In U. S. Steel's South Works below Chicago, for example, the non-English-speaking portion of the labor force shrank from nearly half in 1907 to 37 per cent in 1908. In that depression year, nearly two thirds of the immigrant steelworkers surveyed by the Immigration Commission had been unemployed for three months or more. Every week of idleness depleted savings and postponed their departure to the old country by perhaps twice that time.

When prosperity returned and the labor market tightened, the immigrants struck back. Suppressed resentment, built up during hard times, expressed itself in demands for higher wages and in generalized unrest. After the sharp depression of 1907–09, spontaneous strikes broke out in the Chicago district and at several points in Pennsylvania—most importantly, a serious strike at Bethlehem. Labor leaders began to revise their estimate of the docility of the immigrants. Management, Gompers said, assumes that the foreigners will always accept injustice. "But some day they will protest. . . . If the great industrial combinations do not deal with us they will have somebody else to deal with who will not have the American idea."

At the time, however, the immigrant unrest was not harnessed. The AFL "has undertaken . . . to uplift, educate and nationalize the strangers within our gates. To do this . . . is the problem which we are to solve." But organized labor did not solve it then. Union campaigns had no real success. The immigrants proved to be effective strikers, but poor union men. Nothing in their background made trade unionism entirely comprehensible. What was more, a real conflict existed between immigrant aims and the union belief in a restricted labor market. The AFL surely injured its cause in the 1912 drive by urging steelworkers to advise "your friends and relatives across the water . . . it would be to their advantage if they did not come to America for a year or two."[34] As prosperity continued, the recruits drifted out of the newly formed unions.

The ethnic factor raised another kind of organizing problem. A deep social gap divided the recent immigrants and the English-speaking workmen in the mills. A steelworker told of the hardships of another man in his plant: "But he was only a Hunky, and no decent American would have anything to do with him—for, be it said, we workers have our classes the same as other people." And another skilled man: "The Hunkies? They're only cattle." This bias resulted in the designation of many mill jobs as unfit for Americans. Few skilled workers would move down to immigrant work temporarily at the steel plant in Steelton, Pennsylvania, in 1908; they preferred to be laid off. Anxious to dissociate himself from the immigrant, the American worker identified with the neighborhood shopkeeper and artisan, and with them tended to look up to the mill officials. Social tensions helped attach the skilled men to their employers.

Nativist sentiment undermined trade unionism in a more direct way. Labor leaders had concluded that effective organization in steel demanded the inclusion of all production workers in a single union (as an organizing circular said), "regardless of their mechanical ability, their creed, color or nationality." But to draw in the immigrants, as the AFL deliberately attempted in 1912, meant to alienate the native workingmen. The Amalgamated Association, made up as it was of English-speaking men, lost enthusiasm for organizing work partly for this reason. Moments of crisis—for instance, a strike at McKees Rocks, Pennsylvania—sometimes drew natives and immigrants together temporarily, but no basis appeared for more permanent organizational unity. (Even at McKees Rocks two separate unions were formed.) The trade-union leadership, sharing the nativist inclinations of American workmen, compounded the problem. Gompers saw the need to teach trade unionism to the immigrants—"untutored, born in lands of oppression . . . reaching manhood without that full mental development which makes for independence and self-preservation."[35] But labor leaders were blind to the equally important task of educating Americans in the kind of trade unionism that would offer a place for the immigrant workmen. The omission would exact a heavy price.

For the moment, the seeds of trade unionism fell on barren ground in the basic steel industry. The steelmakers remained unrelenting: they would fight to the limit of their vast resources to preserve the open shop. Organized labor had a commitment and an untried plan of organization, but slender means and little enthusiasm for an unpromising fight. For their part, the steelworkers lived in circumstances that stifled any strong impulse toward organization. Unionization of the steel industry seemed a hopeless prospect.

2

Wartime Upheaval

No ONE could foresee the start of unionism among steel-workers. For it could not happen under normal conditions. As long as management retained its superior power and workingmen their reasons for docility, steel would remain an open-shop industry. A few union leaders—not necessarily those closest to steel—recognized the importance of the mass-production sector for the future of American trade unionism. "To organize the steel industry would be like putting the backbone in the labor movement," said one of the activists. But even they saw no hope "for the workers to accomplish anything by organized effort."[1]

Then the industrial situation altered in entirely unexpected ways. War broke out in Europe, and set in motion forces that created a new opportunity to unionize the American steel industry.

The labor market quickly felt the effect of the European conflict. In early 1915, war orders began to pour in. The business recession that had begun in 1913 ended, and soon the steel mills were running full blast. But the war also shut off the flow of urgently needed immigrants. Industry spokesmen warned that "each month that passes makes the situation as to our foreign-born labor supply just so much more critical, as for many years we had been accustomed to a regular influx." Studying the immigration data, steelmen feared that as a result of "outrunning our labor supply . . . even prosperity may have its bounds."[2]

That dire prospect was averted by a new source of unskilled labor. During the spring of 1916, Southern Negroes began migrating north in large numbers. Initiated by Northern employers, including some steel companies, the migration soon became largely self-sustaining. By November of 1918, approximately half a million Negroes had moved north. They filled the vacant places in the steel mills. When the war ended, Negroes made up 11.4 per cent of the steel labor force in Illinois, 14.2 per cent in Indiana, 10.9 per cent in Pennsylvania. They seemed, however, an imperfect substitute for the European immigrants. The new workers appeared poorly suited to the job demands in steel, had a very high turnover rate, and frequently clashed with whites in the mills. Management, accustomed to the stolid peasantry of Eastern Europe, did not take readily to the black workers. "It would be better," the Inland Steel president said after the war, ". . . if the mills could continue to recruit their forces from [Europe]. The Negroes should remain in the South."[3]

Nor was the shortage entirely filled by the colored recruits. When the United States entered the war, the labor market tightened further. The steel companies were forced to bid against each other and against other industries for manpower, and every day they lost irreplaceable men to the armed services. Steelmen related their troubles at a meeting of the War Industries Board in August of 1918. James A. Campbell of Youngstown Sheet and Tube observed that, from a payroll of 14,000, his company could count on a daily work force of only 12,000. "That is a serious matter. The men want a day off to have a good time for recreation, or for one reason or another. A good many will take a week off and they are ashamed to come back and go to the plant across the river, or somewhere else." Other officials spoke of the draft. Of the 285,000 employees on the U. S. Steel payroll on April 5, 1917, 25,940 were now in service. (The total number for the

J. P Morgan   4266

industry, according to the American Iron and Steel Institute, reached 131,504 by the war's end.) John A. Topping of Republic Steel warned that a forthcoming draft call would hurt his company's operations. "I know we are pretty badly crippled and many of our neighbors are in just as bad shape."[4] Nothing better expressed employer desperation than Judge Gary's remarkable suggestion of January 1918 that Asiatic workers be imported to relieve the labor shortage.

War brought prosperity, and prosperity, as in the past, brought labor unrest. Two severe strikes occurred before the United States entered the war. The first of these began at Christmas of 1915, when the immigrant laborers spontaneously struck at the Republic tube mill in East Youngstown. The trouble spread rapidly through the rest of the Republic complex, and then to the Youngstown Sheet and Tube Company. On the afternoon of January 7, 1916, Youngstown Sheet and Tube Company guards fired into a crowd of strikers, setting off a bloody riot that soon turned against the town. Four city blocks were razed before the Ohio National Guard restored order the following day. Equally serious was the violence in Pittsburgh at the end of April 1916, which grew out of a bitter strike at the Westinghouse works. Seeking to spread the conflict, the Westinghouse strikers marched from plant to plant. Steelworkers joined them, shouting "Eight hours." Bloody rioting broke out on May 2 at the U. S. Steel works in Braddock, and the threat of a general strike hung over the entire Pittsburgh district. But the workers' rage had spent itself, and quiet fell as soon as soldiers arrived and confined the Westinghouse strike leaders. "The war spirit has risen," a steel trade journal warned. "Plant managers have had to face constantly the possibility that any day's demands would put an end to operations."[5]

The steel industry acted quickly to relieve the tension in the mills. Immediately following the labor troubles in

Youngstown in January 1916, wages were advanced 10 per cent. Business was becoming immensely profitable (U. S. Steel earned a record third of a billion dollars in 1916) and, as the New York *Times* piously reported, U. S. Steel's "far-seeing financiers assert that it is nothing less than fair that the workers should share in the profits." But, the *Times* continued, they also saw "that one of the surest ways to avoid discontent and strikes was to let wages mount in advance of living costs." As a result, an unprecedented series of voluntary increases—seven by August 1, 1918—pushed the common labor rate from 20 to 42 cents an hour. The labor shortage also fostered a changed attitude toward the unskilled workers. "That is the labor we are shortest of," observed the president of Midvale Steel, "that is one that is usually given the least attention." Welfare benefits were expanded to cover the immigrant workmen as well as the skilled men. The industry sponsored "Americanization" campaigns, partly from patriotic motives, but also in the belief that, because of the language barrier, "misunderstandings occur, suspicion, race friction, waste and inefficiency interfere with normal industrial production." The immigrants, an executive told his foremen, "ought to have your help to become citizens. These men are needed. . . . Their loyal co-operation and their progress are good things for the company." Once the United States entered the war, management could appeal to the workers' patriotism:

Men of the Gary Mills, . . . you are building the wall of steel that holds back the mailed fists of our enemies. You have broken many production records, there are many more to be broken. Make the sky your limit, the forced peace of the entire world your goal.[6]

The war propaganda, much of it aimed at the recent immigrants, unquestionably made for happier relations and higher production in the steel mills.

The Pittsburgh disturbances of May 1916 gave way to a relatively peaceful period in the industry. Even so, the steel companies could not prevent the trade unions from capitalizing on the labor shortage. The situation, said Samuel Gompers, gave "a slight opportunity for the laborer to choose." "All manufacturing establishments are more or less short of materials and help," union officers noted in August 1917. "The power of victimization has lost its force during a period of intense expansion and inflated prices." To fire a man was no threat "when jobs are begging for men." The unions seized the opportunity. The AFL sent in organizers wherever trouble threatened, as at the Jones and Laughlin plant in Pittsburgh in September 1917. National unions with jurisdiction in steel entered the field. The Machinists moved into U. S. Steel's Southern subsidiary, Midvale Steel, and Bethlehem Steel. Despite the lack of organizing funds, even the moribund Amalgamated Association of Iron, Steel and Tin Workers began to expand in the finishing branches of the industry. Breaking into plants that had earlier seemed impregnable, the Amalgamated grew from 85 active lodges to 133, and the membership from somewhat over 7,000 to 19,000 between May 1915 and May 1918. "In the history of the American trades union movement," asserted the union with renewed confidence, "there was never a better opportunity to organize the skilled and unskilled workers. . . . What is required is a little courage and determination."[7]

That claim actually overstated the case. The favorable labor market differed from earlier shortages of supply only in degree, not in kind. Unionism had not taken hold in basic steel in past periods of prosperity, nor was it doing so now even under the special economic conditions of wartime. While some headway was registered in the finishing fields and among certain craft groups in the steel industry, the plants themselves remained almost wholly

[49]

unorganized; and major steel companies, where they did find unions on their properties, refused to recognize them. By the summer of 1918, in spite of a three-year labor short-age, the steel industry had not been unionized.

Labor's opportunity sprang from an entirely new development. Unionization was, at bottom, a question of power. Wartime labor shortages had altered the balance somewhat, but hardly to the point of overcoming the power of a mass-production industry such as steel. Now, however, the war injected another factor. Military needs demanded full and uninterrupted production. To assure labor peace, the Government intervened massively in labor-management relations that had hitherto been completely private. The action was unprecedented, and so were its results.

"The industrial freedom of wage-earners depends upon their keeping control over industrial relations within their own hands," Samuel Gompers had said in January 1917. "Once delegate even a particle of that authority to the government and they limit their freedom and forge a chain that retards normal free action in all lines. . . . They must retain [economic] power and oppose every effort that would take from them their birthright as free workers—free citizens."[8] This expressed the historic voluntarism of American labor. Within a few months, that doctrine grew untenable. From his place on the Advisory Commission of the Council of National Defense, Gompers perceived that the war would force the Government to take the levers of industrial control. The shrewd AFL leader drew a quick conclusion. Since Government intervention was unavoidable, the labor movement should act to protect its interests and, if possible, turn the emergency to advantage.

Anxious to secure labor co-operation, the Administration accommodated the unions. "I beg you to feel that my support has not been lacking," Woodrow Wilson assured Gompers on August 31, 1917, "and that the government has not failed in granting every just demand advanced by you in the name of the American worker." Organized labor received a full measure of public recognition. One signal honor was the President's unprecedented appearance at the AFL convention in Buffalo in November 1917. The Administration rejected employer demands for emergency measures prohibiting strikes and lowering labor standards. Gradually, too, the AFL made good its demand for a voice on home-front policy. At first, union representation in Government counsels was confined to labor adjustment boards dealing with Government work such as cantonment construction, and shipbuilding. But, under increasing pressure, the Administration placed union spokesmen on other war agencies affecting labor. In May 1918, for instance, Gompers used his considerable influence to persuade Government departments to appoint their union representatives to the important War Labor Policies Board. With three such appointees, he then requested the selection of someone directly from labor's ranks "in order to assure confidence among workers in the policies and activities of the board."

To a visitor to Washington in the winter of 1918, the signs of organized labor's political power abounded: in the office of the Secretary of Labor, waiting delegations of packers and packinghouse workers; at the AFL building, Gompers too busy to see two employers; at the Committee of Public Information office, a bulletin that the President's Mediation Commission was urging a new trial for labor martyr Tom Mooney.[9]

The experience shocked employers. By the summer of 1918, the War Industries Board determined not only the price of steel but also its distribution. Behind this direction rested the real threat of emergency nationalization.

[51]

Steelmen perforce co-operated. Shorn of many former prerogatives, they saw also the despised union chieftains acceding to power and influence in Washington. The Government, one steelman said at an emergency meeting of the industry's leaders in August 1918, "already reserve[s] the right to say what you shall pay for ore, what you shall receive for your product—only one thing remains and that is the terms of labor. That privilege is liable to be taken away." The real problem, Judge Gary added, was that "there is not anyone present who can tell what is going to happen with respect to the labor question, because the Government is very powerful; and sometimes we think certain sections of industry [i.e., labor], are pretty powerful in government circles." Steelmen could only hope, as Judge Gary said before the War Industries Board in March 1918, that the question of labor organization in open-shop industries would "be left out of the discussion and decisions during the war. We must set aside all these differences for the present."[10] At that moment during the second spring of war, the Government was verging on a momentous decision.

Before the war, employers had been free to resist unionization by any means that did not violate the ordinary rules of law. The right to organize and engage in collective bargaining had no legal standing. As the war progressed, the idea began to take hold that workingmen should have such basic guarantees. Secretary of Labor William B. Wilson expressed the thought as early as April 23, 1917. The labor adjustment boards uniformly attacked discrimination against union members. By the start of 1918, the labor movement was openly demanding public protection for union rights. "The cornerstone of our national labor policy must be the right to organize," insisted the AFL. "No other policy is compatible with the spirit and methods of democracy."[11]

In March 1918, the War Labor Conference Board recommended a program to govern wartime labor-management relations. Among the principles enunciated was "the right of workmen to organize in trade-unions" without hindrance "by the employers in any manner whatsoever." Management should further be required to bargain with shop committees, but not with union representatives. For their part, unions should not coerce workmen to join, or employers to bargain or to grant the union shop. The National War Labor Board was created to apply these principles in labor disputes that threatened war production. For the first time in the country's history, workingmen could organize without fear of reprisal.

Trouble had brewed for months at the giant Bethlehem Steel Works in South Bethlehem, Pennsylvania. The machinists and electrical workers complained of increasing hardships: a complicated bonus system that masked systematic rate cutting ("We knew we would soon be working our heads off for nothing if we kept speeding up"); substandard wage and overtime rates; and company discrimination against union men (among other ways, by manipulating the deferment arrangements covering draftable workers). When the machinists sent a committee to the plant office in April 1918, the management refused even to talk with the spokesmen, precipitating a machinists' strike which threatened to spread through the entire works. A month later, with the dispute still unresolved and the machinists ready to walk out again, the National War Labor Board accepted the Bethlehem case.

Arriving at the plant to make a preliminary investigation, board examiners privately urged company president Eugene G. Grace to accept the N.W.L.B. principle of conferring with a workers' committee. "Mr. Grace, however, could not see his way clear to do this," the examiners reported to Washington. "In no uncertain terms he stated that while he was always willing and ready to receive individual employees and adjust grievances . . . he would not deal with a committee who came to him representing men or if the committee in its formation in any way savored—was the word he used—savored of organization then most assuredly the company would not deal with it." At subsequent hearings Bethlehem clung stubbornly to its policy of dealing only with individual workers. "We do not employ a committee, we employ a particular workman and naturally, we are always ready to listen to what he has to say and make corrections."[12] It was a voice out of the nineteenth century.

The N.W.L.B. handed down its decision on July 31, 1918. The company was directed to revise or eliminate its bonus plan, to conform with the minimum hourly rates of the War and Navy Departments, and to pay time-and-a-half for work over eight hours and double time for Sundays and holidays. Other provisions of the award cut deeper. The N.W.L.B. invoked the prohibition against antiunion activities. An examiner would investigate charges of past discrimination, and the War Department would take up the draft problem. The company was ordered to deal with shop committees elected by the employees under the supervision of an N.W.L.B. examiner. Finally, a local board of mediation and conciliation, representing labor and management equally, would deliberate issues left open by the board.

Hostile to the entire proceedings, the company made no move to implement the board's decision. The machinists grew increasingly restive. On September 11, they warned the N.W.L.B. that unless the company complied, they would strike. And if, as a result, "the life of one American soldier is sacrificed . . . we want you gentlemen, members of the War Labor Board, to place the responsibility where it belongs, on the heads of the officials of the

Bethlehem Steel Company." On September 15, Eugene Grace appeared before an angry board. Its decision, he explained, placed a heavy financial burden on the company. He wanted a price increase to cover the higher wages and overtime provisions prescribed in the award. Although guaranteeing nothing, the board agreed to send a request to the War Industries Board. In exchange, Grace promised to act on the rest of the decision. The election of shop committees took place at last.[13]

At first, the steel industry had not been alarmed by the new developments in Washington. The N.W.L.B. expressly protected the open shop and nonrecognition of unions; and the right to join a union had, after all, formed an integral part of the open-shop argument. The Bethlehem case shocked steelmen out of their complacency. The decision, *Iron Age* warned, "directly or indirectly affects labor conditions in the great majority of manufacturing plants that thus far are not thoroughly unionized." The result, steelmakers felt, would certainly be increased labor activity in their plants. Open-shop employers, reported *Iron Age* in September, "are beginning to lose faith in the National War Labor Board" because its decisions "almost unfailingly open the door to and deliberately encourage the unionization of plants that have peacefully operated open shops for long periods."

Stung by such charges, William Howard Taft, the N.W.L.B.'s public co-chairman selected by the management members of the board, defended the Bethlehem decision in a private memorandum. Although it was "being heralded as a new and radical announcement effecting a change in many important industries," this conclusion was "unwarranted," the portly ex-President insisted. "These rulings do not, as has been reported, unionize Bethlehem." Taft was correct in principle, wrong in practice. Was nonrecognition of unions—the core of open-shop doctrine—anything more than a fiction if the unions controlled the shop committees? That was proving to be the result of the committee elections at the Bethlehem plant. And the right to join a union, acceptable to employers in the abstract, became a fearful threat when the War Labor Board stood behind it. Hence this curious protest to the board from the Steel Fabricators of the United States: "The right of workers to join a union is not questioned, but [that] . . . and the right of a national union to institute a country-wide attack . . . are two very different things."[14] The complaint boiled down to the fact that the trade unions, granted the right to organize, were now actually doing so.

A holding action alone held out hope to the steel companies. U. S. Steel, for example, adopted a noncommittal policy of "reserve." During a conference in September 1918 on labor problems in the steel industry, Government representative Felix Frankfurter put a hypothetical question to Judge Gary:

FRANKFURTER: Suppose that in some one of your plants some of your employees should bring a matter of complaint before the National War Labor Board. That is a perfectly conceivable situation. And the War Labor Board should make a decision which of course your company would respect as the decision of a branch of the Government. I assume I am correct in making that assumption.
JUDGE GARY: I could not answer that question just now, and certainly not in the affirmative. . . . A small number of employees in one of my plants might make a complaint to the War Labor Board. We would have to see that that portion of our employees who did not make the complaint were protected. . . . That case might arise and the War Labor Board might make a decision which would affect indirectly all our other plants, and I do not know what I would do under those circumstances. But this is too big a question for us to go into just now.

Judge Gary hoped never to have to go into it. When the N.W.L.B. tried to enter a dispute involving the U. S. Steel sheet and tin-plate subsidiary, the company vice president answered that the matter would have to be decided by the head office in New York. Two months later, in October 1918, the subsidiary president claimed he had not discussed the issue with steel corporation officers because "there is no case here for the board to consider." The N.W.L.B. examiner reported to Washington: "It was absolutely impossible to develop the situation far enough to have them consent to have it come before the board."[15] Time alone would tell how long such evasive action would work. Meanwhile, the War Labor Board was taking on more cases involving steel companies; and, as the Bethlehem case made clear, the board had ample powers to intervene in disputes and to enforce its decisions.

On August 28, 1918, 150 industry leaders gathered at the Waldorf-Astoria to consider a new threat from Washington. In his capacity as president of American Iron and Steel Institute, Judge Gary had been corresponding with the War Labor Policies Board. Its secretary, Felix Frankfurter, wanted Gary to appoint a small standing committee of industry representatives to help develop labor policies for iron and steel. The War Labor Policies Board intended to standardize employment conditions in order "to steady industrial relations." This task, Frankfurter explained, required the active co-operation of industry and labor, "and as I see it the only way to have it is to establish means of regular contact with those who may be affected by the decisions which we will have to make." As examples, Frankfurter cited the building and metal trades, where employer organizations and national unions had already formed committees to confer with the W.L.P.B.

Judge Gary was most alarmed. Besides asking the steel companies to share their power to set labor standards, Frankfurter was implying that they should sit down with unions. The open shop itself was thereby endangered.

The idea depended on the refusal to deal with unions. So long as the steelmakers withheld recognition, organized labor could not take permanent root in the mills. Frankfurter was striking the vital part of the industry's labor strategy. And if the W.L.P.B. determined labor standards, why not also policy on unions? The assembled steelmen suspected a plot by "persons who are perhaps very influential in the governmental departments at this time to organize and unionize all of the iron and steel trade."

Their vague fears actually had some foundation. In the records of the War Labor Policies Board in the National Archives is a three-page typewritten undated document with the penciled notation, "File: Steel Industry Confidential." The first page begins:

> The purpose of the plan is to create in industry a condition of collective bargaining between employer and employee. It contemplates, and is based upon the existence of unions of employees and union of employers. It provides for industrial courts for reaching decisions when agreements cannot be reached. It makes binding and enforceable against both parties the agreements entered into and decisions rendered.

The ambitious plan, developed by someone who was bright and imaginative but obviously without trade-union experience (perhaps Frankfurter himself), was never implemented, nor, for that matter, was it ever revealed.

At the Waldorf-Astoria meeting, the worried industrialists considered the alternatives. They could not resist the immense wartime powers of the Government. "Now, gentlemen, if a fight is made," one man warned, "it is a question whether or not the labor organizations . . . have not power enough to have the U. S. Government take over the iron and steel industries." The meeting placed full discretionary power in the hands of the Iron and Steel Institute's General Committee. Its mission, far from cooperating in Frankfurter's plan, was to avoid so far as possible such involvement and, as Eugene Grace said, "to see whether or not we are going to be able in any way to have a say, so to speak, and protect the relations between labor and ourselves in our own industry."

Three weeks later, a peremptory telegram from Frankfurter summoned Judge Gary to Washington. The tense confrontation on September 20 delineated the changes wrought by war. On one side of the table sat Felix Frankfurter, the young Harvard law professor suddenly thrust into a seat of power; on the other side, flanked by several colleagues, sat Judge Gary, accustomed to ruling within his industry and deeply resentful of his upstart antagonist. The Government, Frankfurter began, was formulating a national policy on the workday. Before making a recommendation, he wanted "the benefit of the experience and judgment of the great basic industry of the country, namely, the steel industry on the question of what should be done." The eight-hour day, Frankfurter continued, was becoming the standard because of Federal law covering Government work, the voluntary action of employers, and the awards of the War Labor Board. Exceptions to that standard disrupted production and labor peace. Frankfurter ticked off alternatives: the Government might reverse the trend toward the eight-hour day, or it could leave the situation as it was. Both he dismissed as "impracticable." Now, what did the Judge suggest?

Gary burst out angrily against the subterfuge. Frankfurter "was not asking really his opinion," but "was practically putting him the proposition that the basic eight-hour day must be extended to the steel industry." The twelve-hour day was a necessity in steel, Gary argued, and the basic eight-hour day (that is, time-and-a-half after eight hours) was "a sham . . . a method of obtaining a wage increase under false pretenses." Then Frankfurter asked casually, to illustrate "the fact that the situation could not

[59]

be let alone," what would happen if a dispute over hours arose in a U. S. Steel mill and came before the War Labor Board. Abruptly, Judge Gary gave in. Though still asserting his opposition to change, he agreed to consult his colleagues in the steel corporation and in the industry. Five days later, the Iron and Steel Institute suddenly announced the adoption of the basic eight-hour day effective October 1. So far as the public knew, the decision was voluntary. But privately Judge Gary let it be understood that his hand had been forced by Frankfurter. (When William Howard Taft queried him about the charge, Frankfurter innocently insisted he had merely solicited Gary's views: "The thing is too absurd on its face. Think of Judge Gary taking so vast a step on my bare say-so!") Still, time-and-a-half was a price the steelmen were willing to pay to forestall the Government.[16]

The war thus worked a marvelous change in the labor affairs of the steelmakers. Certain scenes would remain indelible: imperious Eugene Grace lamely explaining to the War Labor Board why he had not put its award into effect and promising to do better; august Judge Gary being subtly coerced by an obscure liberal lawyer to give up the hallowed twelve-hour day. For once, events were setting heavily against the steelmen. The best they could hope for, Judge Gary remarked, was for labor questions to "be postponed until after the war and until after the difficulties surrounding the war have passed away."[17]

The steelmen's trials were the opportunities of their union adversaries. "The Government stands firmly behind the organized labor movement in its right to organize," asserted the Amalgamated Association, "and that is why it is going to push its work of organization into the steel industries." The power balance had surely shifted. A key unionist afterward summed up the situation in the war months of 1918: "The demand for soldiers and munitions had made labor scarce; the Federal administration was friendly; the right to organize was freely conceded by the government and even insisted upon; the steel industry was the masterclock of the whole war program and had to be kept in operation at all costs; the workers were taking new heart and making demands. . . . The gods were indeed fighting on the side of Labor. It was an opportunity to organize the industry such as might never again occur."[18] It had to be seized.

Saturday, March 30, 1918, was a memorable day in the Chicago stockyards. That morning, Judge Samuel Alschuler had handed down an arbitration award that granted to the packinghouse workers the eight-hour day with ten hours' pay; overtime rates after eight hours; additional pay increases; and other important concessions. The decision culminated the first union breakthrough in a mass-production industry during the war. Swift & Co., Armour & Co., and the lesser packers—defenders of the open shop no less than the steel companies—had been partially organized during the second half of 1917. Failing to gain recognition, the unions threatened to strike. The President's Mediation Commission rushed to Chicago and, early on Christmas morning of 1917, secured a no-strike agreement calling for a Federal Administrator to oversee labor relations in the packing centers and to arbitrate issues that were left unsettled by direct negotiation. Judge Alschuler's decision was the triumphant result.

Two Chicago men were instrumental in the packinghouse achievement. One was John Fitzpatrick, veteran president of the powerful Chicago Federation of Labor. This honest, unassuming Irishman represented the best in American organized labor. "An uncalculating idealism, quite simple, but quite determined, was in him," an observer remarked. Schooled in the craft-oriented, pragmatic tradition of American labor, Fitzpatrick nevertheless harbored a deep sympathy for the immigrant workingmen of Chicago. "When I think of those [steel] trust magnates and the conditions their workers live in and work in and die in—why their hearts must be as black as the ace of spades."[19] The other figure in the Chicago dispute, an enigma where John Fitzpatrick was an open book, was William Z. Foster. A slight, quiet-spoken, intense man in his late thirties, Foster had come out of the darkest Philadelphia slums, knocked about for years as a laborer, sailor, timber worker and railroader, and somehow educated himself. In his younger days an IWW syndicalist, he had become convinced that radical, dual unionism could not succeed in America. He entered an AFL affiliate, the Brotherhood of Railway Carmen, and quickly gained prominence in its Chicago branch. The high order of Foster's talents marked him as a man of promise to AFL leaders. He helped initiate the packinghouse drive in Chicago, and served brilliantly as secretary of the joint union body, the Stockyards Labor Council.

Steel was next. A week after the Alschuler award had eased the packinghouse situation, Foster introduced a resolution before the Chicago Federation of Labor proposing an organizing drive in the steel industry. The resolution was adopted unanimously and forwarded to the AFL headquarters in Washington. Anxious to prod the slow Federation machinery into motion, the Chicago Federation (Foster was its delegate) introduced another resolution at the AFL convention at St. Paul on June 17, 1918, calling for a conference during the convention. Three large meetings were held in the last days of the exuberant convention. "Prospects look good for a big steel campaign," Foster reported to the lawyer who had represented the workers in the packinghouse arbitration. "The greatest confidence prevailed."[20]

Thirty union leaders assembled in Chicago on August 1, 1918. Samuel Gompers, who presided, set the expectant tone of the conference in his opening remarks.

> The old relation in industry of master and slave is giving way to new ones where employer and employe meet on the basis of equality as parties having problems. We have established democracy in politics, now we must establish democracy in industry. Too long did autocracy reign in the packing industry, and among the telegraphs. But this is all changed now. And our present purpose is to establish democracy in the iron and steel industry.[21]

A National Committee for Organizing Iron and Steel Workers was created with "full charge of the organizing work." Each of the co-operating national unions would have one representative. The chairman, who the conference agreed should speak for the AFL, was Gompers. But he was too heavily occupied with his war duties in Washington to devote himself to the drive (in fact, he had to leave before the end of the Chicago conference), so John Fitzpatrick was elected temporary chairman and, in that capacity, actually headed the National Committee. Later he became its regular chairman. No person was better able to hold in harness the independent-minded unions making up the National Committee than the respected Fitzpatrick. William Z. Foster, the man most responsible for the enterprise, was the natural choice for secretary-treasurer. He had already demonstrated his genius as a tactician and organizer in the stockyards. It was an effective executive combination.

The American Federation of Labor was putting to a test its ability to organize mass-production industries without departing from existing doctrines and structure. Remarkable in view of earlier and subsequent agitation, no voice was raised then for industrial unionism. For one thing, the wartime situation seemed too favorable for organizing to be wasted in a debate over structure. Men likely to favor industrial organization—Foster himself, for instance—were anxious to grasp the chance. Moreover, the craft principle had been adapted successfully in the railroad shops and, more directly, in the stockyards. A conservative course, as Foster afterward observed, was "the best fitted to get results at this stage in the development of the unions and the packing industry. And the outcome proved the wisdom of the decision."[22]

Accordingly, no national union surrendered its claim to workmen in the steel industry. Fifteen national unions attended the organizing conference in Chicago on August 1, 1918, and eventually 24 unions participated in the National Committee for Organizing Iron and Steel Workers. Of these, a number were craft unions of the interindustry variety—Blacksmiths, Boilermakers, Electrical Workers, Machinists, and so on. Their jurisdictions covered roughly a quarter of the total labor force, ranging from 8 per cent of the total for the Machinists down to a few hundred men for the Coopers, Bricklayers and Patternmakers. Another group took in workmen on the periphery of the steel industry—Mine Workers, Quarry Workers, Seamen, Foundry Employees. Two unions held residual jurisdictions over all steelworkers unclaimed by other unions. The Mine, Mill and Smelter Workers covered the blast furnaces, and the Amalgamated Association of Iron, Steel and Tin Workers covered the steelmaking (including wrought iron) and finishing branches. The mass of unskilled workers in the industry fell within these two unions.

They had sprung from very different labor traditions. The Mine, Mill and Smelter Workers (earlier the radical Western Federation of Miners) had started in the Western mine fields and had always followed a policy of inclusiveness. The Amalgamated, though it had since 1909 accepted in principle the need to organize the unskilled, in practice had remained limited to skilled workers in puddling and finishing plants. But the war had revived earlier ambitions to recapture the basic steel plants. And that, everyone now knew, required the organization of the unskilled. The Amalgamated, asserted its president in May 1918, "is destined . . . to control the destinies of all men engaged in the manufacture of iron and steel products."[23] This sounded suspiciously like industrial unionism, but, barring a few minor infractions and an occasional hothead, the Amalgamated was content to honor the jurisdictional claims of the other unions. Receiving far more—roughly half of all recruits—than it contributed to the drive, the Amalgamated had no intention of jeopardizing its position.

Jurisdiction was thus arranged, though not without occasional bickering over the maze of craft lines. The Electrical Workers and the Stationary Engineers had a particularly fierce quarrel over the electrical cranemen in the steel mills. These differences, however, do not compare with the kind of explosion that would have followed an attempt to consolidated steel jurisdictions in one industrial union. The disposition of the steelworkers was the best jurisdictional adjustment that could be made within the existing framework of the labor movement. Above all, the unskilled workers now had a definite place in the arrangement. It remained to be seen whether the 24 national unions would accept the responsibility that went with their claims in iron and steel.

The national unions were sovereign within their own jurisdictions, and this autonomy was not diminished in any degree by participation in the National Committee for Organizing Iron and Steel Workers. Membership was entirely voluntary; there were unions—the Carpenters, for instance—that could have participated but did not choose to do so. The National Committee could not order the member unions to provide funds or organizers, to follow a standard policy toward their steel memberships, or, in fact, to do anything that they found disagreeable. Expulsion was the only sanction at the disposal of the National Committee, and, as in the AFL, this would be resorted to only in extreme cases. "This is a federated proposition, and it is a free-will organization," explained Foster. "It is not bound together by any constitution or law or anything, except just common interest. The only way we can maintain that committee together is to have a thorough understanding and agreement among the organizations taking part in it."[24]

Despite this independence, everyone accepted the need for joint effort. The Stockyards Labor Council in Chicago demonstrated the accomplishments possible through common action. When Foster introduced the original resolution for a national steel drive before the Chicago Federation of Labor, the delegates scarcely debated the necessity for a joint enterprise. "We knew how hopeless [it] would be," John Fitzpatrick remarked afterward, for each organization to work alone "against the power of the steel trust." The National Committee embodied the conviction "that it is folly for any craft organization, however strong or skilled, to attempt to organize singlehanded in the iron and steel industry."[25]

Imbued with this basic notion, the co-operating unions departed from past practice in significant ways. Foremost, of course, was the decision to pool organizing resources and to centralize direction in the National Committee. The working details better revealed the extent of the commitment to the common enterprise. A standard application form and a uniform initiation fee were adopted. Three dollars (one of which went to the National Committee) was less than the fee of many of the participating unions, but only three skilled-craft organizations failed to go along with the arrangement, and even they cut their entrance fee substantially for steelworkers. The men were placed in a common pool, then assigned by trade to the appropriate national unions. An efficient record system kept track of the recruit and his initiation payment until he received a membership card from a national union and left the jurisdiction of the National Committee. The local unions in the steel centers, while subject to a parent national union, were also united locally into iron and steelworkers' councils. These, said Foster, "knit the movement together . . . strengthened the weaker unions . . . prevented irresponsible strike action by over-zealous single trades . . . [and] inculcated the indispensable conception of solidarity along industrial lines." Later, districts would be marked off, each under a secretary answerable to the National Committee.

The national unions by no means lost the inclination to control their own affairs. Almost all, for instance, insisted on directing the work of organizers on their own payrolls, which often led to confusion and duplication. Chairman Fitzpatrick never knew how many organizers were in the field, let alone where they were or what they were doing. Nor were the national unions willing to surrender any part of their authority over their members in the steel industry, which meant that the local iron and steelworkers' councils never had any real disciplinary or decision-making powers. Autonomy placed limits on the achievement of "a central organization, functioning nationally and locally." The joint effort, grumbled one official, had "as much cohesion as a load of furniture."

Autonomy posed another, more pressing problem than the habit of independent action. By entering the National Committee for Organizing Iron and Steel Workers, the 24 national unions assumed a responsibility for carrying their share of the effort. But they were also going organizations with memberships and established functions. How was the proper balance to be struck between their obligations to the Committee and to the vested interests within their unions? Perhaps inevitably, labor officials never doubted that their main—in some cases nearly exclusive—duty was to the latter. John Brophy of the Mine Workers, who attended several meetings, remembered that most of the delegates "were concerned with their own craft union fortunes . . . with just how these things could fit into their specialized fields. . . . They weren't much help as a body."[26] Their narrow vision would subsequently have a variety of unfortunate consequences, especially at the hands of the Amalgamated Association.

The Committee's first major failure, and, in retrospect, probably the fatal one, concerned finances. At the Chicago conference of August 1, 1918, the co-operating unions pledged to contribute organizers ("one or more" was the usual vague promise) and to make initial contributions of only *one hundred dollars* each. "This is the biggest job of organizing ever undertaken by working men anywhere," pleaded National Committee leaders the following month, and "if there is to be a reasonable chance for its success, the proper financial support must be given the movement."[27] The appeal resulted in a per capita assessment of five cents, which brought in some money from eleven participating unions. At the close of 1918, the total contribution from organizations representing close to half the membership of the entire labor movement amounted to a mere $6,322.50. Starting with the new year, the 24 unions agreed to pay a total of $5,000 a month, assessed on the basis of delegation strength at AFL conventions. This pro rata system increased the flow of funds to the National Committee (although the financial statements reveal that contributions consistently fell short of the $5,000 mark), and more organizers were assigned to the steel centers. But at the start the National Committee had little money and only a "corporal's guard" of organizers.

The original strategy for organizing the steel industry had to be scrapped. At the Chicago conference, the delegates had debated whether to launch the drive at a single point or simultaneously everywhere in the industry. A national drive clearly had overriding advantages. It would not only maximize the benefits of surprise but would also enable the drive to get a good start before the war ended. The National Committee decided that a steel drive "can be best handled on a national basis."[28] Niggardly financing instantly undercut that large plan. The National Committee had to reshape its strategy, and limit its opening drive to the Chicago district. A fateful compromise had been made.

During the first week of September, 1918, the organizers fanned out through the Chicago steel district. "We have arranged mass meetings to organize steelworkers in South Chicago, Indiana Harbor, Chicago Heights, Joliet and Hammond, Indiana," John Fitzpatrick reported on September 3. "This is the real actual work of laying the foundation of our organizing campaign." The steelworkers responded instantly. "You talk about spirit," a Gary unionist marveled, "why, that is all these men out here are breathing. They have been hungering for the chance to get in, and at last the Macedonian call was answered." The first mass meetings, an official reported, "brought out tremendous crowds and overflow meetings were held in the streets. . . . The campaign of organization in this district is in full blast." By the month's end, Foster was recording that, "owing to the great rush of signing up new members at Gary, Indiana Harbor, South Chicago and Joliet, it has been necessary to place the secretaries of the local organizing committees on salary."[29] Unionization was taking strong root in the Chicago district.

The steelworkers had never exhibited such enthusiasm. Even industry apologists had to admit, as one Pittsburgh "labor" journal said, "the amazing feature . . . that honest toilers are deceived by the most irresponsible claptrap."[30] Clearly, a startling change had occurred in the steel towns.

The transformation sprang partly from the wartime emergency. Waiting to change trains in Bethlehem in mid-October 1918, a War Labor Board official visited the steel works, where he had formerly been assigned during the Bethlehem case. "It would be impossible to overstate the change for the better that has occurred in the morale of these folks," he wrote to his superior. "They seemed in fine fettle and in a mood of great hope coupled with a joyful settling down to the task of electing shop committees."[31] By protecting the right to organize, the War Labor Board had created a confidence hitherto unknown among the steelworkers. The tight labor market, moreover, meant that a man did not risk his livelihood by joining a union. No employer opposition met the drive in the Chicago district. At Gary, fresh recruits immediately pinned on their union buttons; they had to be persuaded not to wear the buttons to work until organization was solidified in the Gary mills. "Brothers, when jobs are begging for men, and the U. S. Government [is] . . . with us," one Cleveland man wrote, "we cannot let this opportunity go by."

Nor did the steelworkers lack grievances. Wage rates had risen rapidly during the war years, but so had the cost of living. While substantial, the gain in real wages was only a fraction of the money increase. According to expert opinion, the annual income of unskilled steelworkers in 1918 fell $121 short of the minimum subsistence level for a family of five. In addition, the work schedule lengthened to meet the pressing labor shortage. The seven-day week, which had been largely abandoned by 1915, reappeared in continuous-operation departments. The twelve-hour day was more widespread in 1919 than it had been in 1911. Yet, on the whole, the steelworker's lot was better. Real income was up. Welfare programs had been extended to a larger part of the work force. U. S. Steel tripled its welfare expenditures between 1915 and 1918. And the industry shrewdly appealed to patriotism to turn aside resentment over speed-up and long hours. ("Our country needs us now. This is the time to show your loyalty. Are you one of us?")[32]

The war worked a special change on the immigrants. Earlier, the immigrant workingmen had fixed their eyes on the Old World rather than on the alien life of industrial America. They would return to the home village, they thought, as soon as they saved enough money. Their plan made pointless the risks of a fight for labor organization and collective bargaining. But the war, interrupting the population flow between the Old World and the New for four years, held the immigrant in America. Simultaneously, new circumstances encouraged the immigrants' commitment to the United States. Ironically, management was mainly responsible. Anxious to reduce turnover and discontent, steel companies pushed "Americanization" programs to "cement the people in our country into a homogeneous nation."[33]

When America entered the war, the immigrant steelworkers began purchasing Liberty bonds, serving in the Army, and, above all, turning out war matériel. Parades, speeches and noon-hour rallies stirred patriotic sentiments in the mill towns. Such activities, U. S. Steel president James A. Farrell told a subordinate, would arouse "a sense of patriotism without which we might have difficulty in carrying on successfully the work before us." Production needs drove the patriotic appeal to an emotional peak. Captain J. C. Curran of the Emergency Fleet Corporation harangued the steelworkers of a Cleveland plant:

"Those boys over there in France [are] laying down their lives for you and me; my message to you men is today for God's sake to support those boys by staying on the job and by working. . . . My friends, I have got a message for you direct from your government . . . that your greasy overalls . . . are as much a badge of service and honor in . . . the eyes of your country today as the uniform of the army or navy.

"In looking over this sea of faces I notice that quite a number of you come from lands beyond the sea. You are welcome in America, no matter what country you come from. But . . . remember this much, as you have all the privileges of the native-born American, you have likewise the same obligations. . . . You are expected to fight by their side, and if you are not willing to do that, then damn you, go back to the country from whence you came."[34]

The immigrants were indeed willing; the proof was in production records broken during the war. (At Homestead, the men labored so feverishly that during a heat wave in the summer of 1918 the plant superintendent had to caution them against overstrain.) The experience recast many of the immigrants' basic assumptions. By the end of the war they felt themselves *of* as well as *in* America. The change fulfilled the prime precondition for the unionization of the Hunky workmen. They were affected in another way by the war. It invested the trade unions with a deeper appeal than derived from being (in Gompers's phrase) "the business institutions of the wage earners."

The Federal Administration, perceiving at the outset the need for popular support for the war effort, mounted an unprecedented propaganda campaign. The Committee of Public Information intended to reach "every community in the United States by written or spoken word or motion picture," George Creel told President Wilson, "until every individual, native, naturalized, or alien, has it seared into his consciousness that this is a war of self-defense, and that it has got to be master of his every thought and action." Not even in the grimy industrial towns could men escape the voice of Washington. Chief among the propaganda arguments was the claim that the United States was crusading to make the world safe for democracy. Steelworkers read in the Homestead *Messenger* that they had to do "their best to help the boys over in France who are fighting for Democracy and freedom and equality for all."[35] That message, constant and ubiquitous, captured the mind of America's industrial workers.

The labor movement seized the democratic line as its own. "If this war is waged for the destruction of political autocracy, we demand . . . the elimination of industrial autocracy in this country. The workers demand a voice in the conditions of their service, in all sections of the country; thus shall they be assured that this is indeed their war." War aims were thereby coupled to the purposes of trade unionism. Organizers carried the compelling message to the steelworkers. "Now is our time to build an industrial army to be able to demand full democracy that the suffering and dying are fighting for on the battlefields at this moment." Thus one unionist summarized the speeches at a Cleveland mass meeting in early October 1918. The steel drive told men they had a duty to buy Liberty bonds, to work hard *and* to join the union. Those who "won't try to get collective bargaining from the steel trust are not even first-class Americans," asserted one union official. By the same token, company resistance seemed, in the words of U. S. Steel employees complaining to the N.W.L.B. against the management of the Elwood, Indiana, mill, "Hun-like . . . autocratic . . . operating here in the same stupid manner that the propaganda and intelligence service of the Wilhelmstrasse operates."[36] So the organizing drive drew for its appeal not only on the promise of better conditions, but equally on powerful patriotic and ideological sources.

Management knew the same trick. Its appeals subtly linked loyalty to company with loyalty to country, exploiting the strain of wartime thinking that stressed the defense of America against its enemies at home and abroad. The Illinois Steel Company (a U. S. Steel subsidiary) asked its employees, in October 1918, to sign a "Pledge of Patriotism" against "any action that would tend to disturb the good relations that have for years existed between the Joliet Works Management and ourselves" and for "loyalty to our country and to the company for which I work." Simultaneously, steelmen identified the union cause with subversion and un-Americanism. An editorial from a local paper was tacked to the bulletin board of the U. S. Steel mill at Elwood:

> There are agitators prowling about the mills . . . spreading German propaganda for the conversion of foreigners especially. . . . These I.W.W. and Socialist vermin, working under the guise of A.F. of L. organizers, teach that the war is bad. These strangers are Liars and German propagandists, some of them probably in the Kaiser's pay.

An Amalgamated organizer complained "of the very scandalous attacks that are being made against us by local newspapers and by the Four Minute Men who are talking at the local theaters on behalf of the Third Liberty Loan. It is evident that the Steel Trust officials are [using] Patriotism as a cloak to drive us out of the city."[37]

Thus, two patriotic appeals competed for the steelworkers' attention in the organizing drive. The industry's chauvinistic line had some impact on susceptible native Americans. The immigrants, themselves foreigners, could hardly flock to an argument strongly antiforeign in its tone. Instead they were readily drawn to the literal ideal-

[74]

ism of the democratic argument. It was the immigrants who really gave the impetus to the organizing drive. They crowded the union rallies and joined up enthusiastically. Their response, said William Z. Foster, "compared favorably with that shown in any organized effort ever put forth by workingmen on this continent. Beyond question they displayed trade-union qualities of the very highest type." The English-speaking steelworkers, in contrast, reacted with greater caution. "The average American should be ashamed of himself for his lack of interest," grumbled one organizer assigned to Gary.[38] Still, if the Americans lacked enthusiasm, they did tend to join after the first rush of immigrant recruits. And, in places such as Bethlehem, Cleveland, and Pueblo, the skilled, English-speaking men did initiate organization.

Encouraged by rapid advances in the Chicago district, the National Committee broadened its attack in the second month of the drive. On October 6, Cleveland had its first mass meeting. The campaign spread to Johnstown, Pennsylvania, to Wheeling, to the Ohio steel towns. When news of the Eastern successes reached Pueblo, Colorado, organization started spontaneously in the Colorado Fuel and Iron Company. Meanwhile, independently of the main drive, unions experienced "most remarkable success" at the Bethlehem Steel Company after the decision of the War Labor Board. But the instant success of the Chicago campaign was not quite duplicated elsewhere. The basic eight-hour day, which went into effect on October 1, 1918, cut some ground from under the union appeal. Then the flu epidemic struck, preventing meetings in many towns during October and November. Nevertheless, at the end of 1918 "good movements" were reported at many production centers outside the Pittsburgh district. "The fruit is ripe and ready to pick," a unionist from West Virginia advised. In the Chicago district, organization was nearly completed. And the National Committee had moved its headquarters from Chicago to Pittsburgh on October 1, 1918, preparatory to an assault on the core of the industry. "Beyond all question the steel industry is being organized," Secretary Foster concluded on January 4, 1919.[39]

But by then the war had ended. On November 17, 1918, Bethlehem Steel president Eugene Grace talked bluntly to a War Labor Board examiner. The company needed a free hand to meet peacetime conditions; Bethlehem considered itself no longer bound by the board's decision. The incredulous examiner retorted that the War Labor Board would insist on the fulfillment of its award. He reminded Grace that Bethlehem and the Federal Government had secured high production and labor peace "through the summer and autumn, largely by reason of the expectations created by this Award." Grace shrugged off the obligation. His company would not pay "arsenal rates," and if the N.W.L.B. wanted the back-pay provision met, it could find the money itself. As for the shop-committee system, Grace wanted it supplanted by his company's own collective-bargaining plan. Grace was in deadly earnest. Immediately, Bethlehem pressed for the removal of the examiner. The shop committees, running smoothly only days before, were now entirely ignored or treated perfunctorily. Notwithstanding a N.W.L.B. ruling, many committeemen were discharged during the production cutback. On December 6, the examiner reported blackly to Washington that the company was "deliberately promoting disintegration of the committee system of the National War Labor Board."[40]

No one could mistake the meaning of the events at Bethlehem. The wartime binds had dissolved, and the steel giant was flexing its muscles. Hardened by the unhappy war experience, steelmakers prepared to resume the fight against trade unionism. They would unhesitatingly throw their full resources into the defense of the open shop.

The war was over for organized labor too, and it had scored only a partial victory in steel. "It could as well have been on a national scale," Foster speculated afterward, "had the international unions . . . put the original plan into execution. . . . The entire steel industry would have been captured for trade unionism and justice."[41] Now the National Committee for Organizing Iron and Steel Workers would have to proceed in the teeth of employer opposition. It would be an unenviable task.

3

Confrontation

AMERICAN STEELMAKERS emerged from the war determined to prevent the unionization of their industry. So much was clear. Yet they were aware, as Judge Gary remarked, that there was a "wave of unrest in certain localities . . . which in our own private circles we have no right to shut our eyes to," and they knew that the unions would try to capitalize on "the abnormal condition of the [steelworkers'] mind." Steelmen had excellent sources of information on such matters. The Steel Fabricators' Association had, in fact, circulated among its members—with appropriate warnings—a copy of Gompers's call for the Chicago conference that would launch the steel drive. Faced with an undeniably real union threat, the industry began to fight back.

On January 21, 1919, the subsidiary presidents of United States Steel gathered for one of their periodic meetings at the corporation's executive offices in New York City. Labor problems were uppermost in everyone's mind. "It has always been our policy to keep ahead of trouble," Judge Gary lectured. "And in keeping out of trouble there is nothing we can do better than to be sure we are liberal in the protection of our workmen and their families."

Make the Steel Corporation a good place for them to work and live. Don't let the families go hungry or cold; give them playgrounds and parks and schools and churches, pure water to drink, every opportunity to keep clean, places of enjoyment, rest and recreation.

[78]

"Take care of your men," the Judge urged his subordinates. "It will cost some money"—a million and a half dollars a month at that time—"but I do not think that is very important in comparison." For fair treatment would leave "no just ground for criticism on the part of those who are connected with the movement of unrest."[1] It was an affirmation of Gary's long-held views on labor relations.

So was his influence on the side of wage stability after the Armistice. A price drop seemed likely, and as Gary's close associate, George W. Perkins, said on November 3, 1918, "if that be so then wages must come down and when that attempt starts I think we will have our hands full to avoid serious trouble." When steel manufacturers met on December 9, 1918, to consider postwar problems, Judge Gary argued that the industry "should not make reductions at the point of wage rates; sacrifices must previously be made by employers."[2] Aided by the slightness of the price decline, Gary won his case. No general wage cuts followed the Armistice.

"Abundantly fair" as Judge Gary desired to be, he still failed to win "confidence and loyal support by our action." Too many corroding grievances remained. For one thing, the industry did nothing about the twelve-hour day and the seven-day week. Despite some concern among steel corporation heads, reform was stymied by a lack of sympathy among operating officials and by technical difficulties, particularly in ending the twelve-hour day. Judge Gary himself admitted privately that "the Sunday work at our factories was not exactly in the condition I had supposed existed, nor up to positive instructions which we had issued." Bitterness among the workers in the steel mills mounted. "It's bad to work such a long day," interviewers heard repeatedly. Just coming off a twenty-four hour "long turn" on his open-hearth furnace, an Italian third helper heard an investigator say that the men made "pretty good money." He replied with quiet passion: "To hell with the money! No can live." "Eight hours and the union" was the slogan of the organizing drive.[3]

Other problems were even less susceptible to management solutions. The companies could stabilize wages, but not living costs. Real wages declined more than 10 per cent during 1919. And unavoidable production cuts followed the Armistice. Extensive unemployment at Bethlehem, wrote a N.W.L.B. examiner in January 1919, "is breaking the grit of many and arousing much bitterness and anger among others." Full production resumed only in the spring of 1919. Time-and-a-half after eight hours, a reform brought on by the war, was hardly sufficient to silence grumbling over long hours, living costs, and unemployment.

Disillusionment quickly crept in. The steelworkers had expected rewards for their wartime sacrifices. "The justice of the demand for a fairer share has been established," one union man insisted in February of 1919. "It is not going to be given up now that the war has ended." One Bethlehem worker, laid off and waiting for his back pay under the N.W.L.B. award, recalled how hard he had worked in response to Government appeals and the promise of improved conditions. "But as to *Present* conditions, the Bethlehem Steel Company [says] we will not pay [the back pay]. . . . Now why is it that the Bethlehem Steel Company is more powerful than the Government?" The answer was clear enough. The workingman "knew that the war was over."[4]

Welfare work could not assuage the deepening sense of grievance. Although no one denied the value of sanitary facilities, safety devices, visiting nurses, or profit-sharing and pension plans, these were not enough to keep workers from feeling that employers "have given us a rotten shake." The paternalism of welfare, in addition, was peculiarly damaging at a time of excitement over industrial democracy. When U. S. Steel decided on a wage increase during the summer of 1918, George Perkins pointed out a "remarkable thing" to his friend Theodore Roosevelt. "A Finance Committee and Board of Directors of a great corporation sat down around a table and acted in a dividend question and a wage question at the same meeting without hearing any more from the labor which they represent than they did from their stockholders, as to what action they should take . . . and as a result of their deliberations acted with what seemed to me equal regard and consideration for both." Why was policy so made? "The employers, the capitalists, those having the highest education, the greatest power and influence," Judge Gary observed to subordinates, have the responsibility to see that "the workmen and their families are appropriately and efficiently cared for," while "drawing the line so that you are just and generous and yet at the same time . . . keeping the whole affair in your own hands."[5]

Even steelmen were calling the paternalistic way into question. Industrial-relations ideas, a product of the scientific management movement, had spread during the war, partially owing to concern over the high labor turnover. At the meeting of U. S. Steel subsidiary presidents in January 1919, two U. S. Labor Department experts described the advantages of personnel-management methods. Annoyed by some of their remarks, Judge Gary dismissed the concept as a "fad," and it had little effect on the steel corporation. But elsewhere in the industry industrial-relations policies were taking hold. The trade journals began publishing numerous articles on the subject; companies hired experts and set up personnel departments. Unlike old-fashioned welfare policy, the fresh approach emphasized the "human element": the workman's mind had to be considered as well as his physical needs. The most forthright critic of paternalism within the industry, W. B. Dickson of Midvale Steel and Ordnance, likened U. S. Steel's labor policy to "industrial feudalism . . . with a high degree of comfort and safety for the worker, I grant you, but none the less, feudalism."[6]

This new reasoning led ultimately to employee representation or, as trade unionists called it derisively, company unionism. Youngstown Sheet and Tube Company, vice president C. S. Robinson related, had for years supported welfare benefits and profit-sharing, "not . . . as a charity but in a spirit of helpfulness." He and his associates eventually concluded that the company's expenditures were not purchasing the good will of the employees. In 1916 an industrial-relations department was formed to study the problem, centralize labor activities, and receive employee complaints. Still dissatisfied, Robinson looked into the employee representation plan of the Colorado Fuel and Iron Company. John D. Rockefeller, Jr., chief stockholder in the company, had introduced the experiment there after the Colorado coal strike of 1913–14 that had ended in the dreadful Ludlow Massacre. The steel industry paid close attention to the results of employee representation at Colorado's steel plant at Pueblo, and some steelmen—Robinson among them—were inclined to accept Rockefeller's claim that the plan was "a vital factor in . . . developing a genuine spirit of brotherhood" within the company.[7]

Employee representation gained popularity during the World War. For one thing, abnormal conditions opened employers' minds to new ways of handling labor affairs: old methods had obviously broken down. "Industrial democracy," moreover, had an appeal not confined to trade-union circles. "In our free America the day of the autocratic employer has passed, never, I hope, to return," asserted Midvale Steel's W. B. Dickson at the end of the war. "The idea of industrial democracy [is] in harmony with the ideals upon which our Government was founded, and for which the world has agonized for the past four years." For steelmen, employee representation embodied this wartime idealism. But the plan exerted also a narrower attraction. The National War Labor Board required employers to deal with their employees through shop committees rather than trade unions. Open-shop companies seized on the loophole. Thus the typical advice of an employers' association: "As collective bargaining is sanctioned by the Government we advise the employers to treat with the men in their employ. . . . Be sure that the shop committee is of your best employees and not a committee appointed by outside agencies." An employee representation plan, if protected from union infiltration, promised a safe defense against interference from Washington. And, into the bargain, it might even cut the appeal of trade unionism. That, *Iron Age* said, would "depend upon the success of the producers of steel in winning their workmen to industrial democracy, as represented by the new plan."[8]

By early 1919, employee representation functioned at Bethlehem, Midvale, Youngstown Sheet and Tube, Lukens, Inland, and some lesser firms. Among the big independents, Republic and Jones and Laughlin remained unconvinced. But the vital holdout was U. S. Steel. Judge Gary rejected the new-fangled idea. In March 1920, John D. Rockefeller, Jr., sent George Perkins a confidential report on employee representation at Colorado Fuel and Iron. "My own feeling is that if our mutual friend will take the time to read such a report, his whole attitude in regard to the value and importance of introducing such a plan would change."[9] But Judge Gary was not to be persuaded. He was committed to his welfare philosophy.

He thought employee representation infringed on property rights; if workers wanted a voice in management, they should become stockholders. And he doubted that it would work—that is, foster loyalty and contentment. In this last regard, the Judge was right.

Certain plans suffered from the cynical motives of their sponsors. Bethlehem Steel, which had adhered to a policy of individual bargaining until its troubles with the War Labor Board, was a case in point. In October 1918, the company abruptly introduced an elaborate plan of employee representation. At the main works in South Bethlehem, however, union-dominated shop committees had been elected under N.W.L.B. supervision. The company wanted to replace them, using its own representation plan. Eugene Grace so informed the War Labor Board soon after the Armistice (an earlier attempt had been peremptorily refused). The angry board rose up in arms against this transparent move. Stung by a public rebuke from Co-Chairman William Howard Taft, Grace backed down, and, on February 4, 1919, agreed to negotiate a new plan with the existing shop committeemen. For its part, the board would remove its examiner from the plant, although not relinquishing jurisdiction in the case. Taft, however, refused to withdraw his criticism of Grace unless a N.W.L.B. examiner remained at South Bethlehem: "With that security for performance I would have been glad to make the statement. . . . I felt that I had to await the working out of the plan in good faith." On those terms, Grace preferred to let the "stigma" stand for the present.

The negotiations for a representation plan proved difficult, aggravated as they were by dismissals of committeemen during production cutbacks. The company, a union leader charged, was trying "to make it easy to install [a] company union." Finally, with N.W.L.B. representatives again present, a plan was adopted on April 3, 1919, which, at least on paper, gave employee representatives an unusual measure of independence. In addition, the shop committeemen chosen earlier would continue as members of the General Committee (the highest representative body in the plant) for one year after the first election. The Bethlehem steelworkers had, in the end, benefited from the company's ineptitude. But they had no reason to believe in its good faith, and they would strike to abolish the representation plan when the occasion arose.[10]

Sincere advocate of the principle though he was, William Dickson of Midvale Steel also blundered in his handling of employee representation. It took the intervention of the War Labor Board in a dispute at Midvale's Nicetown plant to prod him into revealing a plan, which he later claimed to have had under consideration for many months. Sprung on unprepared men, the first election chose foremen as a majority of the representatives (to Dickson's chagrin). Unionists could only conclude that "it is a hoodwink . . . for the sole purpose of trying to deceive the War Labor Board." Midvale's "industrial democracy" became entirely farcical when the employee representatives, meeting in Atlantic City at company expense on a hot August day in 1919, resolved that a chief cause of the high cost of living was "the persistent and unceasing demand of workmen . . . for a shorter day's work and an increased wage." This action, Midvale assured the public, "was in no way influenced by the officials of the company" and represented "the thought and ideas of their fellow workmen." At the company's Cambria Works in Johnstown men felt otherwise. Despite a warning against absenteeism on Labor Day, throngs of steelworkers joined the union parade carrying defiant signs: "We are for the shorter day and more pay." The Atlantic City meeting, chortled a labor journal, was the "suicide of a company union."[11]

No matter how well administered, employee representation fell short as an alternative to trade unionism. The

[85]

company schemes varied in detail and even in scope. At the least, individual grievances could be aired. Some plans permitted consideration of the substantive issues of wages, hours and conditions. At the Colorado Fuel and Iron Company, the employee representatives persuaded the management to adopt the eight-hour day. But however close to the form, employee representation never had the substance of collective bargaining. "We discuss matters, but we never vote," Charles Schwab of Bethlehem Steel confided later. "I will not permit myself to be in a position of having labor dictate to management." Public statements were more delicately put, but the basic premise was everywhere the same. Employee representation therefore could not satisfy steelworkers. In November 1919, Ben M. Selekman, a staff member of the Russell Sage Foundation and later a major figure in the industrial-relations field, arrived in Pueblo to study the pioneering plan of the Colorado Fuel and Iron Company. The employee representatives, he reported, "felt that . . . they were impotent. . . . When they went into conference . . . they felt ineffective and powerless. They had no backing. The men were not organized, and the representatives could make no threat which would give force to their demands. Under the plan, they said, it was simply a matter of taking what the management was willing to give them." Admitting the honest intentions of the company and the benefits deriving from the plan, the workers preferred to face management on an equal footing; they wanted economic power and professional representatives.[12]

By the test that truly mattered to steelmen, employee representation patently failed. Wherever such plans existed, the unions flourished. And where management blundered, as at Johnstown, organization spurted forward.

In the postwar months, the steel industry acted on the assumption that it could immunize steelworkers against trade unionism by meeting their needs. The validity of that assumption was untestable. For time-and-a-half and stable wages, welfare work and employee representation did not amount to a "fair shake" to the men. The industry could only resort now to tougher methods. Could the steelmakers achieve by force what they had failed to do through welfare and company unions?

The Armistice had freed the hand of management. The public prohibition against union discrimination was no longer in force, nor was the pressure for continuous war production. Yet steelmakers took little action against unionists in subsequent months. Men reported spotters at union halls and other signs of company displeasure, but there were few cases of discharge. As the organizing drive continued, however, the apparatus of repression moved into higher gear.

In February 1919, Midvale officials took advantage of production cutbacks to fire union activists at the huge Cambria Works in Johnstown, Pennsylvania. Secretary Foster reported to the National Committee for Organizing Iron and Steel Workers that the company had suddenly "declared war on the unions. During the past few weeks hundreds of union men have been discharged point-blank. The company are [*sic*] pursuing a policy of frightfulness. They are picking out and discharging the oldest employees they have who belong to the unions. . . . Many of the men have from 10 to 35 years in point of service." At a special meeting held in Johnstown on March 8, the National Committee demanded that the company end discrimination and reinstate all men already laid off "out of order of seniority." Otherwise, the unions would fight. "Every effort should be used to prevent a strike, but if it is forced upon us we must meet it," concluded the Molders' representative. "It is better to die fighting than to die without having had the courage to strike a blow in your own defense." A three-man committee departed for Washington. Assistant Secretary of Labor H. L. Kerwin, who had already sent an ineffectual mediator to Johnstown, dispatched another man from the Conciliation Service to New York City with the committee to appeal to leading steelmen. The result of these efforts was a promise from Midvale to the Department of Labor that it would not discharge men for joining unions, but the company would make no reinstatements. Still, it was enough. The National Committee felt that "this changed attitude on the part of the company relieved the situation somewhat."[13]

It was a hollow victory. Discrimination soon resumed at the Cambria Works, and then spread throughout the industry. By the summer of 1919, antiunion measures were in general evidence. The Gary *Union News* reported that "company officials are picking out men here and there for the pink slip and invariably it is a union worker of some consequence." This was the experience—one among many in several hundred collected affidavits—of Joe Mayor of Homestead, Pennsylvania:

Mayor said that he had worked for the Carnegie Steel Co. in the car wheel shop 12 years and had never been discharged before.

He joined the union on August 5th [1919]. He was discharged August 15th by Supt. Munle, who called him into his office but [*sic*] said "Were you at the meeting Tuesday night?"

M.—I was. How do you know?

Supt.—Somebody turned your name in and I am going to discharge you.

M.—What's matter? What I do, rob company of couple of dollars?

Supt.—We don't want you to attend union meetings. I don't want union men to work for me.

When the Superintendent inquired what they had told him at the meeting, he refused to answer and further refused to answer when the Superintendent asked him for the names of others present at the meeting. The Superintendent then called a policeman and he was taken out of the shop.

M. got a job for two weeks under a different name, as he knew himself to be blacklisted. Is a citizen and married; has lived in Homestead 14 years.[14]

So the steelmakers brought to bear the weapons of discharge, blacklist and espionage. In early September 1919, the National Committee received reports that "the companies are discharging the men by the hundreds."

Yet, as practiced in 1919, repression had this failing: it was not ruthless enough. With few exceptions, steelmen advocated the open shop, which meant, among other things, freedom to join a union. "We never ask the question," Judge Gary insisted. "We have known that we have a good many union men, of course. While it has been said we discharged them . . . there is no foundation for that statement. If that . . . has ever been done, which I deny, it has been contrary to our positive instructions." Dismissals without cause were easy enough to explain away. "We don't discharge a man for belonging to a union," U. S. Steel officials emphasized, "but of course we discharge men for agitating in the mills."[15] Still, the public—perhaps even private—commitment to open-shop doctrine acted as a brake on discriminatory practices. So did the idea, born of the war experience, that union membership was a right worthy of public protection—witness the appeal to Washington in the Midvale case. Though it doubtless discouraged the fainthearted, coercion was too belated and mild to uproot the organizing movement. Rather, its chief result was to render unionists angrier and more impatient.

There was yet another way to counter the union drive. If the steelworkers could not be reached, they could not be unionized. For a time, no obstacles were placed in the way of organizers appearing in the steel towns. They moved freely in the Chicago district, and in the secondary centers of the industry. But a wall met organizers entering mill towns in the vital Pittsburgh district. At Homestead, J. G. Brown hired a hall, then checked with burgess P. H. McGuire (a veteran of the great Homestead strike who had long since been converted from unionism).

[89]

He said, "Well, you cannot hold any meetings at Homestead."

I said, "Why not?" He said, "In the first place, you cannot get a hall."

"Well," I said, "we have a hall. We have got a hall, all right."

"Then," he said, "what do you want of me?"

I said, "We want to arrange to have a band play on the street and distribute some advertisements."

He said, "There will be no bands play on the streets of Homestead and no advertising done."

I said, "Well, now, could not we pass cards around to the houses or something of that sort?"

"No sir," he said, "you cannot pass anything in any way."

"Could we not advertise in the papers?" I said.

"Oh, yes," he said, "if you want to; if you can get the space. I don't think you can get the space."

So the matter dropped at that, and the next morning I was called and told that a mistake had been made, that the hall had been rented to someone else. . . . They very much regretted the proposition, but they would have to cancel that lease.

Organizers had similar experiences elsewhere in the Pittsburgh district. The National Committee immediately realized that it had "to establish the right of assembly in Pittsburgh, or no hope of success could be expected in this campaign."[16]

The fight focused on McKeesport. Situated a few miles up the Monongahela River from Pittsburgh, McKeesport was the site of several large tin mills and a major works of U. S. Steel's National Tube Company. Under a local ordinance, a permit was required to hold public meetings, and the mayor of McKeesport, a martinet named George H. Lysle, had in the past used this power brazenly against the trade unions. In April 1918, the Amalgamated had tried to organize the Port Vue tin mill. Not only did Lysle refuse the union a permit, but borough police watched indifferently as the Port Vue superintendent beat up one organizer and cursed the others. Recalling the company thugs planted at the railroad station, one union official remarked, "I would study a long time if I had a choice of getting off at Berlin or McKeesport."[17] When the national drive reached McKeesport in November 1918, Mayor Lysle once again denied permits for union meetings.

The National Committee tried a reasonable approach. Representatives appeared before a regular session of the McKeesport City Council on November 25, 1918. They "explained at length the purpose of the American Federation of Labor, the dangers of suppressing free speech and free assembly, and fully presented the right of Organized Labor to have a hearing in McKeesport." The city council listened in silence, and then Mayor Lysle started on other business. The one union man on the council, the president of the McKeesport Trades Council, hastily moved that a permit be granted for steelworkers' meetings. The motion did not receive a second. The National Committee representatives returned to the local union headquarters to consider their next move. Legal recourse would be expensive, slow, and, in view of previous court decisions on local regulation of public assembly, probably futile. The National Committee did decide to hire "some first-class lawyer," but in the end, it relied mainly on public pressure.

The unions had a powerful case against McKeesport. "Does the U. S. Constitution apply to Pennsylvania? Is the right of assembly fundamental or is it a thing to be granted or withheld at the whim of every petty official?" In those postwar months the AFL was at the peak of its prestige: "A fine way to treat the representatives of the organization our most worthy President lauded for its contributions to win the war. Some democracy!" The week after the McKeesport City Council meeting, a committee led by John Fitzpatrick left for Washington to get the support and advice of AFL leaders. The Secretary of Labor and the

Governor of Pennsylvania agreed to see what could be done. But their efforts were lukewarm. The Labor Department started an investigation, but did not follow it up or even issue a public report. The governor merely expressed faint disapproval. Apathy toward labor's troubles foreshadowed trouble ahead; the Red scare was not far off. "The free speech deadlock still persists," Secretary Foster had to report in mid-February 1919.[18]

Yet these were not wasted months. The free-speech issue kept union sentiment alive in the Pittsburgh area, but the agitation there, Foster later admitted, was really diversionary. Limited in resources, the National Committee was concentrating its real organizing activities outside the Pittsburgh district where it was free to reach the steelworkers. By the early spring of 1919, the drive had made considerable progress. Union strongpoints surrounded western Pennsylvania. The National Committee was stronger now, and production was picking up in the industry. It was time to break into the Pittsburgh district. The mill towns within it were closed tighter than ever. Many, following the example of McKeesport, had adopted ordinances requiring permits for public meetings. Only a frontal assault would serve. The National Committee formed "The Flying Squadron," a group of seven or eight organizers whose job it was to get into the steel towns and hold meetings, law or no law.

The first targets were the towns of Monessen and Donora in the heart of union coal country about forty miles from Pittsburgh. A mass meeting in Monessen was scheduled for April 1, 1919, with speakers to include such labor luminaries as the indomitable Mother Jones, President James Maurer of the Pennsylvania Federation of Labor, President Philip Murray of Mine Workers' District Five, and others. The burgess threatened to prosecute violators of local ordinances, but he caved in when thousands of union miners marched into town for the meeting.

Monessen was open territory after that. Donora was harder to crack. For several months a resourceful Mine Workers' organizer named William Feeney, the district secretary of the National Committee, held meetings on a mountainside edging Donora. When local businessmen warned Feeney to leave town, the union miners answered with a tight boycott, forcing Donora merchants to apologize to Feeney. The burgess bowed to pressure from commercial interests and the growing steel union. Once he began to issue meeting permits, organization quickly sprang up in Donora's large American Steel and Wire plant.

Closer to Pittsburgh, lacking the support of mine workers, the Flying Squadron aroused public opinion and inflamed the steelworkers, so that, as the National Committee hoped, town officials could "not stand in the face of it."[19] On May 19, 1919, the first street meeting ("as it was impossible to hire a hall") was held in notorious McKeesport. Despite his public warnings, Mayor Lysle made no move to interfere, and meetings were then scheduled for every Sunday afternoon. Doubtless to save face, Mayor Lysle finally agreed to issue permits if meetings were conducted in English, and lists of speakers were submitted to him in advance. Both conditions were ignored in practice. So the slow, tense fight proceeded. Some places, Rankin for instance, were relatively easy to open. In others, speakers were locked up and fined. The leader of the Flying Squadron held the record for arrests—eight times during the drive.

Actually, police interference dramatized the union cause to great effect, especially if Mother Jones happened to be one of the offenders. This white-haired old lady (she claimed to be 89) was a veteran agitator full of fire and invective. "We are to see whether Pennsylvania belongs to Kaiser Gary or Uncle Sam," she thundered in Homestead on August 20, 1919.

[93]

Our Kaisers sit up and smoke seventy-five cent cigars and have lackeys with knee pants bring them champagne while you starve, while you grow old at forty, stoking their furnaces. You pull in your belts while they banquet. They have stomachs two miles long and two miles wide and you fill them. . . .

If Gary wants to work twelve hours a day let him go in the blooming mill and work. What we want is a little leisure, time for music, playgrounds, a decent home, books, and the things that make life worth while.

The Homestead police promptly hauled her off to jail. Her audience followed ominously. Mother Jones had to come out of the jailhouse to pacify the indignant men and tell them to go home.[20] The threat of such incidents overawed local authorities. With or without permits, union organizers held their meetings during the spring and summer of 1919.

Yet the drive fell short in the Pittsburgh district, where mounting union success stiffened the companies' resistance. By late August, the barriers against union meetings were going up again. When Rabbi Stephen Wise of New York City asked to talk on behalf of the union cause, the mayor of Duquesne shot back: "Jesus Christ himself could not speak in Duquesne for the A.F. of L.!" Town officials were responding to influence from the mills. At a Senate hearing, the superintendent of the Carnegie mill in Duquesne, A. F. Diehl, blurted out who pulled the strings in his community.

MR. CHAIRMAN: What happened to the [proposed union] meeting?
MR. DIEHL: Well, *we* simply prohibited it.
MR. CHAIRMAN: The authorities prohibited it?
MR. DIEHL: On the ground that they said they were going to hold the meeting without having a permit.

There were some company towns, among them Aliquippa, Midland, Weirton, West Virginia, that organizers hardly dared to enter. Tom Girdler, who was to become famous during the 1930's as the antiunion head of Republic Steel, was in 1919 the superintendent of the Jones and Laughlin works in Aliquippa. When an organizer stepped from the train one day, two silent men became his shadows. The organizer left town in a few hours. After that, Girdler recalled with satisfaction, the unions caused no trouble in Aliquippa.[21]

No doubt the Flying Squadron could in time have broken through to the steelworkers. But the unions did not have time. For them the issue was rushing to a crisis. "The dam broke before this district was more than half worked," a Pittsburgh organizer admitted.[22] The steel unions would have to fight with the key industrial district partially and unreliably organized.

The steelmakers could not counteract the union tide. Neither benevolence nor repression dissuaded workers from joining unions. That failure was, however, in itself inconclusive. What mattered was not whether or not men joined the union, but whether the steel companies would deal with the union. The key issue was recognition. Without it, the successes of the National Committee for Organizing Iron and Steel Workers would be meaningless and transitory. And recognition resolved itself into a question of power. "We are not obliged to contract with unions if we do not choose to do so," Judge Gary pointed out.[23] Labor leaders still hoped that public pressure could sway the steel "autocrats." If not, then only the sheer force of labor organization might win recognition from the industry.

The National Committee now discovered a cruel irony. The very conditions that stimulated the organizing campaign cut it short before the unions developed the strength to push the steel companies to the bargaining table. The impatient steelworkers would not wait until their unions were ready to confront the industry. Discontent boiled up in the mill towns. The workers felt betrayed. The country was forgetting "that we have strained every muscle to keep up production and render service to our government in winning the war." "The justice of the demand for a fair share has been established; it took the war to do it but it is not going to be given up now that the war has ended. . . . A few millions of wage-earners have been fighting for certain principles that have become quite firmly impressed in their minds . . . namely democracy not only in government, but in industry." And what did the steelworkers find?

An impotent War Labor Board unable to dispose effectively of the backlog of cases at the end of hostilities: "It looks as tho the War Labor Board has gone on a vacation, as their promises are still unfulfilled and some of them were unloaded altogether. . . . The boys have become disheartened, as they worked faithfully, thinking that the board was sincere and that their case would be settled in a quick and satisfactory manner." And from a spokesman of Bethlehem workers still waiting for their back pay in May 1919: "As matters now stand, the men feel that everyone connected with the War Labor Board had double-crossed them."

Working conditions that seemed harder than ever (in the broken English of one Homestead worker): "We did not have the right conditions, and we were only paid forty-two cents an hour, and we worked like a mule, and if you ever say anything to them they will discharge you, and you don't have a word to say. We were never treated right while we were there."

Employers who scorned the union version of "industrial democracy": "It is almost beyond the conception of the ordinary citizen's mind that employers would continue to assume the arrogant, overbearing attitude toward their employees that they do."

And, lastly, discrimination against union members: "This is the United States and we ought to have the right to belong to the union."[24]

Demands for action poured into the National Committee from the steel centers. "Already the men are restless and anxious for something to be done," Committee members warned at a session on April 5, 1919. No one wanted "the movement to go off half-cocked. . . . We must look out not to get them started into action that might catch us unprepared." A workers' conference with no authority to make decisions might "pacify the restless spirits." "It would be merely a plan to give the men who have waited so long something tangible to look forward to. It would operate to hold the men in line better and to make them wait more patiently." So the National Committee decided to call a general conference for May 25, 1919.[25]

That Sunday, 583 men gathered at the Labor Temple in Pittsburgh. They represented South Chicago, Youngstown, Birmingham, Bethlehem, and every other steel-making center where organization had taken hold. Most of them were rough-handed steelworkers ignorant of the intricacies of trade unionism. But they did know all too well what they were up against in the steel mills. They came armed with resolutions and instructions, expecting to decide on a concrete course of action. They listened to reports of local conditions and organizational progress. They introduced resolutions calling for free speech in the Pittsburgh towns, the eight-hour day "or less," an end to discrimination against union men, and the abolition of company unions. If the steel companies refused their demands, "a general strike [should] be called." Many men felt that "the attitude of the employers is so hostile that strong action must be taken to withstand it, even if a strike should be necessary."

Union functionaries were dismayed by this display of rank-and-file militancy. John Fitzpatrick hastened to emphasize that this was only "a general get-together meeting," designed to find out "the sentiments of the great bulk of the members and . . . the needs of the various localities." The conference lacked power to make any binding decisions, for such action would "be an infringement upon the rights of the International Unions, these organizations, in the final analysis, being the supreme authority in their respective trades." The National Committee urged the delegates to be patient. But, as the tense day wore on, experienced unionists saw that some kind of positive move was demanded. So a substitute resolution was offered requesting the unions affiliated with the National Committee "to enter into [joint] negotiations with the various steel companies to the end that better wages, shorter hours, improved working conditions and the trade union system of collective bargaining be established in the steel industry."[26]

The Pittsburgh conference had backfired against the National Committee. Far from damping the unrest, the meeting crystallized the sentiment for action. The National Committee was not eager to approach the industry. Less than two weeks before, Judge Gary had denied a request by the Amalgamated Association of Iron, Steel and Tin Workers, acting independently, for a conference with U. S. Steel: "As you know, we do not confer, negotiate with, or combat labor unions as such. We stand for the open shop." Although it had no reason to expect a more favorable response, the National Committee dared not ignore the directive of the Pittsburgh conference.

On June 20, 1919, Samuel Gompers sent a letter to Judge Gary. The steel drive, Gompers explained, had already recruited over 100,000 men and had "exceedingly bright" prospects for complete success. The AFL, he assured Gary, sought "better conditions for the toilers, by American methods, and American understandings, not by revolutionary methods or the inauguration of a cataclysm." Would the Judge therefore consent to a conference with a committee "representing not only the iron and steel workers who are organized, but representing the best interests of the unorganized men in the employ of your Corporation?" The National Committee received its answer from Gompers on July 8: Gary had ignored his letter. (Afterward, the Judge, who prided himself on his good manners, justified the discourtesy by claiming that the Amalgamated Association had distorted his letter of the previous month to suggest a change in the policy of the steel corporation, with an "effect . . . bad upon the minds of our men . . . some of them joined the union.")[27]

Rank-and-file pressure was becoming explosive. "All over the entire steel district the men are in a state of great unrest," Secretary Foster reported to the National Committee on July 13. "Great strikes are threatening unless some means are found to prevent them." The next week, he read a telegram from the Johnstown Allied Mill Workers Council: unless a national strike was immediately authorized, "we will be compelled to go on strike alone here." Resentment flared now against the National Committee, and dues payments dropped sharply. Men were "taking the position that they will pay no more dues until they can see some results from their efforts." Either way—spasmodic strikes or mass desertions—"would lead speedily to disruption of this campaign."

So the delegates faced the harsh alternatives. They appreciated "the great power of the United States Steel Corporation and the risk of undertaking a struggle with it without thorough preparation." But they also saw "the danger . . . of our standing idly by and allowing the steel movement to drift out of our hand and to degenerate into an unorganized uprising." Inaction, they knew, was the greater danger. To move against the steel industry at least offered a slender possibility of success. On July 20, the National Committee debated whether to take a strike vote. Everyone agreed that a premature test of power was likely to result. But "oftentimes the only way men can be held is by taking such a vote, and . . . in this case it is practically the only hope." The motion passed, twelve unions for, two against.[28]

Since each union polled its own membership, the balloting consumed an entire month. Actually, no one was in any hurry. The National Committee expected the strike vote to stimulate organizing activities. In fact, a special ballot was circulated among unorganized workers inviting them to register their votes at local headquarters. The results exceeded all expectations. At the end of the voting period, the National Committee noted that "the organizations everywhere are experiencing an unprecedented growth. In the Pittsburgh district they are coming in by hundreds daily." And the unions "are taking in thousands of dollars in back dues and initiation fees. There can be no question but that the entire body of steelworkers is profoundly interested in the present movement and intend to give it active support, should it be necessary to bring the mills to a standstill."[29] The vote itself was tabulated on August 20, 1919. The national unions reported percentages, not actual numbers. (This method had been suggested by the National Committee as a precautionary and tactical measure.) An estimated 98 per cent favored (in the words of the ballot) "stopping work should the companies refuse to concede . . . higher wages, shorter hours and better working conditions." There could no longer be any doubt that the steelworkers wanted to stand up to the industry.

At its meeting on July 20, the National Committee had adopted a set of twelve demands to serve as the basis for negotiations:

1. Right of collective bargaining
2. Reinstatement of all men discharged for union activities with pay for time lost
3. Eight-hour day

4. One day's rest in seven
5. Abolition of 24-hour shift
6. Increase in wages sufficient to guarantee American standard of living
7. Standard scales of wages in all trades and classifications of workers
8. Double rates of pay for all overtime after 8 hours, holiday and Sunday work
9. Check-off system of collecting union dues and assessments
10. Principles of seniority to apply in the maintenance, reduction and increase of working forces
11. Abolition of company unions
12. Abolition of physical examination of applicants for employment

The strike vote gave the unions the power to call their men out if the steel industry refused to negotiate. Before fixing a strike date, the National Committee gave itself ten days, from August 20, to get the companies to the bargaining table.

At 3:00 P.M. on Tuesday, August 26, 1919, three businesslike men entered the U. S. Steel offices at 71 Broadway. They identified themselves as John Fitzpatrick, William Z. Foster, and D. J. Davis, representatives of the National Committee for Organizing Iron and Steel Workers, and they asked to see Judge Gary. The secretary returned with a message from the Judge. He did not care to interview the gentlemen personally. If they desired, they could state their business in a letter. This, Gary told reporters after the trio's departure, "would be received and considered by our officials, who would decide what, if any, answer to make. . . . It is better . . . to leave no chance for misunderstanding in regard to what has been or shall be said. I have intended no personal discourtesy."

The letter arrived, containing a request for a conference, and Judge Gary promptly rejected it. He doubted that the labor leaders were authorized to speak for the majority of his employees; he believed in the open shop "which permits one to engage in any line of employment whether one does or does not belong to a labor union"; and he observed that, in labor matters, "the Corporation and subsidiaries have endeavored to occupy a leading and advanced position among employers." The National Committee immediately did what it had expected to do all along; it gave Judge Gary an ultimatum. If he did not change his mind within a few days, "there will be no discretion left to the committee but to enforce the decree of your employees whom we have the honor to represent."[30]

The National Committee had not quite exhausted the alternatives to a strike. Steel organization had begun under the aegis of the Government. Massive public intervention in labor relations had ended with the Armistice, it was true, but the Government had not returned completely to its earlier hands-off attitude. Precedents had been set, and labor crises afflicted the country during "reconstruction." In fact, at the very time of the exchange with Judge Gary, President Wilson was stepping into a dispute involving the railroad shop crafts. During the debate over the strike vote, Chairman Fitzpatrick had prophesied "that the taking of this vote would create such a situation that the Government would intervene and see to it that the steel barons be brought to time, even as the packers were. . . . President Wilson would never allow a great struggle to develop between the steelworkers and their employers."[31] As soon as the National Committee representatives had posted their ultimatum to Judge Gary on August 27, they hurried off to Washington.

The Executive Council of the AFL was in session when they arrived. Detailing the events of the past days to the assembled labor chieftains, John Fitzpatrick suggested that President Wilson be asked to intervene. Gompers, recently returned from an international labor conference in Amsterdam, was glad to demonstrate his influence in the White House. He arranged a meeting with the President for the next day, August 29, and accompanied the steel committee. The group was closeted with President Wilson for forty-five minutes. After describing the situation, the labor men asked him to arrange a meeting with U. S. Steel officials. That, they assured him, was the only point at issue. Wilson was obviously sympathetic. He asserted (Gompers related immediately afterward to the AFL Executive Council) "that the time had passed when any man should refuse to meet representatives of his employes and that he would do what he could to comply with the request." The labor leaders, for their part, promised not to strike during Wilson's intercession with Judge Gary.[32] They left with high hopes; the President was on their side.

That same day, in New York City, Bernard Baruch spoke to Judge Gary in circumstances far different from the many meetings between them during the war. Then, as head of the War Industries Board, Baruch had been armed with the President's emergency powers; on one occasion he had forced Judge Gary to agree on steel prices for war orders by threatening Government seizure of the industry. Now, as the President's emissary in 1919, Baruch could only transmit Wilson's desire for a conference. Judge Gary explained his reluctance. The unions represented a small minority of his employees, adequate machinery existed to handle grievances, and no trouble threatened (as the President's secretary Joe Tumulty transmitted the information to Wilson) "except that which is the result of an attempt on the part of the American Federation of Labor to unionize these shops, an effort they have been making for years and in which they have been unsuccessful." Furthermore, Gary had proof in the form of a canvass that, if a strike did come, it would be opposed by more than 85 per cent of U. S. Steel employees. Baruch tried again on September 9, but Judge Gary remained firm. "He regrets more than he can say," Baruch reported, "that he is unable to change his position and he regrets it more because the request comes from a man for whom he has such great respect."[33]

Wilson accepted the rebuff silently. Once, some days later, he betrayed his anger at employers who refused to confer with employees: "They are wrong and dare not talk things over." But Wilson decided against a public rebuke of the steel industry. For one thing, he was preoccupied with the fight over the League of Nations. Shortly after his interview with the union representatives, Wilson left on his ill-fated national tour in support of the Versailles Treaty. Baruch himself warned that "a most embarrassing position might result because it would bring acutely to the front at this time a new issue which our enemies would use to embarrass the League of Nations fight." Nor were there clear formal grounds—either in law or precedent—on which the President could force the steel magnates to meet with union leaders. The New York *Times,* citing the historic principle of voluntarism, said in an editorial that both sides "must manage their own affairs . . . and cannot appeal to other authority to make special decisions in their favor. Both sides know their lawful rights and should be left to them."[34] So an expectant nation—the steel crisis was by now making headlines—waited in vain for the President to speak out against the steel industry.

Ten agonizing days had passed with no results from Wilson's intercession. The National Committee had to move. On September 9, the presidents of the member unions gathered in Washington to decide on some definite plan. Four days earlier, Tumulty had wired that the President was discouraged but still trying to secure a conference. On September 10, in response to an urgent wire from the assembled union leaders, he sent a second telegram essentially repeating the first. Late that day, the

National Committee set and sent out a strike date: September 22, 1919.

In the papers the next morning, committee members read with astonishment that President Wilson was asking the unions to postpone action for three weeks. An Industrial Conference of labor, management, and public representatives would convene on October 6 to consider postwar labor problems. The President wanted the steel strike postponed, pending the outcome of the Conference. A series of odd mischances had kept the National Committee in the dark about this possibility. Baruch had come up with the postponement idea on September 9 when he had informed the White House of Gary's final rejection of a conference. Yet Tumulty had given no warning to the National Committee in his telegram the next day, perhaps assuming that the unions would continue to delay because of his assurances that the President was still trying and remained hopeful (neither in fact being true). When he did send the request for postponement hours later, Tumulty wired Gompers rather than the National Committee. Since Gompers happened to be in Massachusetts attending his father's funeral, he did not receive the telegram until the morning of September 11. Actually, however, Gompers already knew about the postponement plan. He had talked to Baruch in New York on September 9 (the same day Baruch had seen Gary), had discussed utilizing the Industrial Conference, and had promised to exert "influence to have all demands held over until that time."[35] Yet Gompers, too, had not kept the National Committee informed. In the meanwhile, the strike machinery had started. Now, if the President's request was to be met, the momentum would have to be reversed. The irony cut still deeper. Secrecy had veiled Wilson's dealings with Judge Gary, preventing a public outcry when the steel magnate rebuffed the President.

On the other hand, Wilson had acted openly with the National Committee; his request made headlines across the country. If the strike was not postponed, the blame would rest on labor. The resort to the White House had boomeranged.

When he received Tumulty's telegram, Gompers immediately urged the National Committee to comply. He was, in truth, relieved. The week before, he had warned the National Committee "of the power of the steel trust, its ruthlessness and the glee with which it would deal Labor a heavy blow." An open-shop conspiracy was plotting to force the fight on organized labor at its vulnerable point, and so break its power nationally. The steel crisis was "incomparably the most important facing organized labor." President Wilson's intervention gave the National Committee added cause for caution. Gompers pointed to "the strategic advantage which would accrue from complying with the request of the President, and the great disadvantage which would result if the President's request was flouted." Gompers's view found widespread support. After hearing from the Federation chief, seven national union presidents informed the National Committee that they favored deferment. Newspapers carried reports of the imminent postponement of the strike.[36]

Closer to the scene of action, the situation seemed very different. The strike date had been fixed, and the steel towns were electric with strike talk. Only solid assurances, Fitzpatrick wired Gompers on September 12, could possibly hold the aroused steelworkers in check:

 Any vague, indefinite postponement would mean absolute demoralization and utter ruin for our movement. It would be a thousand times better for the entire labor movement that we lose the strike and suffer complete defeat, than to attempt postponement now, except under a definite arrangement which would absolutely and positively guarantee the steelworkers substantial concessions. If these things cannot be guaranteed, then, in our opinion, our only hope is the strike.

When the National Committee met in Pittsburgh on September 17, a pile of telegrams lay on the table. From Youngstown came the warning that the AFL had to stick to the strike date: "Otherwise the men will strike regardless of any postponement and we will lose control of the situation." Other telegrams carried similar messages. Committeemen attending the session described how the workers felt: "The situation is so tense now in the steel districts that it would be absolutely dangerous for our organizers to go in there to meet the men if the strike is called off. The companies have long carried on a campaign calculated to discredit the A.F. of L. as weak and timid. . . . Should the strike be now called off the men would swallow their arguments whole and make short work of the organization. And then, even if the strike were officially postponed it would not prevent the walkout. Long before . . . any[thing] could be expected to be achieved from the October conference, the unions would have degenerated so much as to be utterly incapable of action, and the A.F. of L. would have suffered the greatest defeat in its history." The vote carried, twelve to three, to abide by the strike date.[37]

Everyone admitted privately that steel could not be beaten in a strike. Gompers told Fitzpatrick of "instance upon instance . . . of enthusiasm and impetuosity of unorganized [men] in driving their movements to destruction . . . all to no purpose." He held this viewpoint till the end. There was, however, even less point in trying to put off the strike. For the steelworkers were not experienced and disciplined unionists able to accept orders and bide their time. They were, as the local secretaries reported, "determined to strike at least one blow at the steel corporations and we will be unable to stop them." That militancy, to Gompers's everlasting chagrin, prevailed "even against the best judgment of the experienced men."[38]

The steelmen, for their part, were willing to see the shutdown come. Their industry had never experienced a national walkout, nor could they believe that their workers were aroused enough to stage one. On September 16, Judge Gary telegraphed his subordinates to hold to U. S. Steel's settled policy of treating "everyone, without exception . . . justly and according to merit. . . . Our employees may be threatened and abused in the effort to influence them to join the union against their own desires; but . . . we should proceed with the conduct of our business in the usual way and should give evidence to our employees that we mean to be fair with them." He was confident (had he not so assured the President?) that "large numbers of our workmen are not members of unions and do not care to be." Other steelmen banked on their company unions. The Colorado Fuel and Iron Company considered its men "so well satisfied with the Industrial Representation Plan that only a few would respond to the national strike call."[39] The industry could not believe that the National Committee could mount an effective strike.

That was not, in any case, the material point. Steelmen considered the struggle worth while at any price. For the dispute was not over wages, hours or conditions, but over unionism itself. Organized labor was demanding the right to represent and bargain for the steelworkers. The industry could not surrender on that point without surrendering managerial prerogatives. The Colorado Fuel and Iron Company, its president explained to the people of Pueblo two days before the strike date, was willing to consider any of the twelve union demands that involved terms of employment, but it could not compromise on "whether or not trade union agreements should displace the industrial representation plan."[40]

During the war, this hard line had actually eased in certain quarters of the industry. A few steelmen, caught up by the wartime fervor, had seemed more sympathetic to trade unionism. One was Bethlehem's Charles Schwab, who, as head of the Government's shipbuilding activities, became famous for his stirring speeches depicting the "reconstruction" of the American social order after the war. The intervention of the War Labor Policies Board in the steel industry—the most harrowing of Judge Gary's wartime experiences—had originally been suggested to Felix Frankfurter by none other than Schwab. Another such figure was W. B. Dickson of Midvale Steel. In March 1919, a N.W.L.B. examiner related an interview with Dickson:

He is a man of big, liberal ideas regarding labor. He believes in unionism, but says he disapproves of some of the acts of the leaders. He was against Gompers until the war came on; now he is a Gompers man. He thinks Gompers and the union men behaved gloriously during the war crisis.

Dickson says the collective bargaining leaven is spreading and that within ten years it will be the rule in all plants and that profit-sharing by workmen has got to come. He says the day when a steel corporation, for example, will produce forty millionaires and forty thousand underpaid workmen—slaves—is gone forever in America.

Impressed but skeptical, the examiner asked whether he regarded employee representation as a substitute for trade unionism. "No," Dickson replied. "I would be perfectly willing to have the union swallow it up, if the union could run it to the advantage of the men in the shop and in fairness to the company. My doctrine is not narrow."

Nothing came of the postwar attempts to capitalize on the enlightened ideas of these men. A month after the Armistice, the AFL organizer at South Bethlehem reported negotiations in progress in New York between Schwab and the federation "by which the Bethlehem Steel Company was to recognize the Unions." This actually happened at the company's shipyards, but not in its steel mills. As for Midvale Steel, when its conservative president A. C. Dinkey left in the early spring of 1919, the National Committee approached the new head, A. A. Corey, who had expressed ideas similar to Dickson's. After some confusion, he rebuffed the union attempt to enter negotiations.[41] The afterglow of wartime liberalism had a short life.

In those tense September weeks, the National Committee approached only U. S. Steel, assuming that Judge Gary spoke for the entire industry. If anything, in fact, most independents probably exceeded the steel corporation in determination. A knowledgeable reporter close to industry leaders, Arundel Cotter, later wrote that many steelmen watched "with some misgivings" the maneuvering for a conference with U. S. Steel. They feared "that the Judge, realizing his immense responsibility, might allow himself to be persuaded into a compromise." Here, possibly, was foreshadowed the split which would occur between Big and Little Steel in 1937. But in 1919 U. S. Steel stood firm, and the industry rallied behind Judge Gary. When he entered the ballroom of the Hotel Commodore in New York to chair an industry meeting on October 24, a noisy demonstration broke out among the sedate members of the American Iron and Steel Institute. "It was a tribute to his generalship in the struggle then being waged," Cotter remarked.[42]

The larger business community solidly backed the industry. Buyers of steel pledged their support. One company, urgently short of roofing sheet, assured its supplier it would gladly wait a year, just so no concessions were made to the unions. The National Council for Industrial Democracy, composed of employers' associations, urged its members to stand behind Judge Gary: "The future industrial destiny of this country is dependent to the greatest degree on . . . the maintenance of open shop." Charles Piez, who had headed the Emergency Fleet Corporation, added that the steel trade "was the last barrier against complete and final unionization of American industry." And from London no less a personage than J. P. Morgan, Jr., cabled Gary:

Heartiest congratulations on your stand for the open shop, with which I am, as you know, absolutely in accord. I believe American principles of liberty deeply involved and must win if we all stand firm.

The steel barons, no less than the labor chiefs, could not yield on the vital issue of union recognition.[43]

And so the strike came. On board his train in the West, President Wilson remarked that he had tried his hardest; now he could only maintain order and let events take their course. In the steel towns, both sides made frantic preparations. The sheriff of Allegheny County deputized loyal employees of the steel companies for strike duty. The state constabulary took up posts throughout the Pittsburgh district. The National Committee broadcast 200,000 strike announcements.

IRON AND STEEL WORKERS! A historic decision confronts us. If we will but stand together like men our demands will soon be granted and a golden era of prosperity will open for us in the steel industry. But if we falter and fail to act this great effort will be lost, and we will sink back into a miserable and hopeless serfdom. The welfare of our wives and children is at stake. Now is the time to insist upon our rights as human beings.

STOP WORK SEPTEMBER 22

And Judge Gary spent a quiet Sunday, September 21, in his country house out on Long Island.

4

The Steel Strike: Public Event

Monday, September 22, dawned gray and rainy in Pueblo, Colorado. At the main entrance of the steel works, officials of the Colorado Fuel and Iron Company waited expectantly for their employees. Outside the plant, men milled around. But they were intent on picketing, not making steel. Scarcely 300 of the 6,500-man force reported for work, and the strike committee even had to furnish maintenance men. Company President J. F. Welborn had been content to await the test: "All the men on the outside on Monday will be yours and all those on the inside will be mine." Now Mr. Welborn had his answer.

So did steelmen in industry centers across the country. At the huge Lackawanna plant outside Buffalo, company representatives had predicted a bare 15 per cent would strike; union organizers had hoped for 70 per cent. To the surprise of both sides, the walkout was almost complete. The Youngstown district secretary said "the success of the first two days is beyond belief." The steel plants were silent, or nearly so, in Wheeling, Gary, Johnstown, Cleveland, Joliet, South Chicago, Milwaukee, and many smaller centers.

The Bethlehem Steel Company, where organization had developed independently of the main union drive, was not struck on September 22. While the Bethlehem unions lacked recognition, they had made some use of the employee representation plan. However, this was not enough once the national strike came. The Bethlehem men demanded abolition of the representation plan and full recognition of the unions. The company refused to discuss these demands. The National Committee would have preferred that Bethlehem maintain production (among other things, this would have applied competitive pressure against the struck companies). Local leaders themselves favored a compromise, "but this is not the feeling of the men." On September 29, the Bethlehem men struck, effectively at the main plant, less so elsewhere.[1]

The strike was far from complete. In the Lehigh Valley and the South, production hardly slowed. In the Pittsburgh district—the key to the entire industry—some plants closed down entirely, for instance at Donora and Monessen, but elsewhere the strike response was mixed or, as at the Carnegie-Duquesne Works and the Jones and Laughlin mills, nearly nonexistent. During the first week, pig-iron production in the Pittsburgh district fell by roughly three-eighths. But output soon picked up again, and was only one-eighth lower in October than in August. For the industry as a whole, October pig-iron production was a third below normal.[2]

The National Committee claimed 275,000 strikers out on the first day, and 365,000 at the strike's peak at the start of the second week. Actually, available information permitted only the roughest estimate, and the union figures were undoubtedly exaggerated. The actual number of strikers was probably somewhere around 250,000—about half the industry's work force. This estimate would fit with the reported tonnage decline of one-third in October, since the industry was straining its operating plants and reopening some struck mills. The walkout was only partial. But still it exceeded in magnitude and scope anything in the nation's experience: a quarter of a million or more steelworkers across the country simultaneously on strike! America had never seen the like of this.

It was indeed a rank-and-file movement. Many more

men came out—probably double the number—than had actually joined a union during the organizing drive. The strike was impelled, as union officials had insisted beforehand, by pressure from below.

More than grievances over wages, hours and conditions actuated the steelworkers. They were responding to their war experience, to the time of high-minded sacrifice when a crusade was being waged to make the world safe for democracy. The betrayal after the Armistice, evident on every side, was climaxed by Judge Gary's refusal to confer with the union representatives. His stand made a mockery of the industrial democracy promised during the war. A strike was necessary, the union at Lebanon, Pennsylvania, explained to the local citizenry, because the steel companies "still persist in their un-American efforts to impose the iron will of the autocrat upon their employees." President Tighe of the Amalgamated asked: "Shall the steelworkers of America, the land of the free, live and die in industrial bondage, and hand down to future generations a heritage that will enslave them?" The strike continued the struggle for democracy on the home front. "Expectancy fills the air," wrote a Gary worker two days before the strike, "and the zero hour draws near. . . . The signal to 'go over the top' is awaited with a quiet confidence that bespeaks the justice of our cause." "The past obedient slaves of the U. S. Steel Corporation are . . . fighting for a share of the profits of reconstruction and . . . democracy," proclaimed another millworker from Elwood, Indiana.[3]

The steelworkers proved, once and for all, that a national strike could be mounted against a basic industry like steel. The industry tried to minimize the impact of the strike. Company spokesmen disputed the numbers claimed by the National Committee, particularly in the Pittsburgh district. They argued that many men feared strike violence, or, having worked steadily and accumulated large savings, welcomed the strike as a lark. Nor did steelmen fail to point out that the strike response was greater among both the less skilled workers and the recent immigrants—the dispensable and "unreliable" elements in the industry. But these arguments could not explain away a strike of more than half the production workers in steel.

"The steel corporation said that the committee representing or assuming to represent the employees of the corporation did not represent any appreciable number," Gompers emphasized. "Well, how could it be demonstrated that they did represent the men? Surely a vote could not be taken . . . but the men rushed right out on strike."[4] The unions had won the opening round. Could this be converted to larger ends? Could the strike achieve union recognition from the steel companies?

The unions had balked when President Wilson had proposed a truce until the Industrial Conference. Now they instantly sensed a chance to turn the Conference to good use.[5] The strike, then at its peak, demolished Judge Gary's claim that the union cause lacked popular support and basic grievances. The case for recognition, thus strengthened, could be pressed in the Industrial Conference. The unions had an arena for bringing public pressure to bear on the steel industry.

Fifty-seven American notables gathered on October 6 in the lavish Pan-American building in Washington, D. C. They were there, as President Wilson had explained in his invitations, to devise ways of resuming, after "the wastages of war . . . the natural course of our industrial and economic development." The country had to end "the wastefulness caused by the continued interruption of many of our important industrial enterprises by strikes and lockouts." Wilson was seeking the advice of three major interests: there was a Public group, chosen by Wilson himself, a Labor group, chosen by the AFL and railroad brotherhoods, and an Employer group, chosen by several management organizations. Together, they would "canvass every relevant feature of the present industrial situation, for the purpose of enabling us to work out, if possible, in a genuine spirit of co-operation a practicable method of association based upon a real community of interest which will redound to the welfare of all our people."[6]

President Wilson had intended the Industrial Conference to operate at the level of generality—to consider the basic principles which should govern American industrial relations. But the raging industrial war was uppermost in everyone's mind. "The existence of the steel strike had the effect of focusing interest and attention upon present conflict," the chairman of the Public group, Bernard Baruch, reported afterward to President Wilson. On October 9, immediately after the preliminaries of the conference, the Labor group launched a dual attack. First came a resolution referring the steel controversy "for adjudication and settlement" to a committee of six chosen by the three groups in the Industrial Conference. Pending a report, the strikers would return to work without prejudice. Another resolution stated labor's rights:

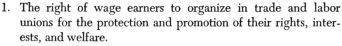

1. The right of wage earners to organize in trade and labor unions for the protection and promotion of their rights, interests, and welfare.
2. The right of wage earners to bargain collectively through trade and labor unions with employers . . .
3. The right of wage earners to be represented by representatives of their own choosing in negotiations and adjustments with employers . . .

The first resolution would create the machinery for settlement and end the strike before it passed its peak. The second resolution would guide the committee of six to a decision that would satisfy the essential requirements of the unions: recognition and collective bargaining from the steel industry. "It was a bit of audacious labor politics, fine strategy from a labor standpoint," Secretary of Interior Franklin K. Lane, chairman of the Conference, complained to the President, ". . . but demoralizing to the whole movement of the conference as a creative body, because it forced the conference to consider the matter of settling a strike before it had time to consider the cause of strikes."[7]

The Labor resolutions incorporated the elements for a smashing union victory against the steel industry. That was painfully clear to Elbert H. Gary, who was attending the Conference as a member, strange to say, of the Public group. "Then for the love of Mike who will represent the employers?" the *Mine Workers' Journal* had asked. In reality, Judge Gary had more cause for chagrin than did his trade-union critics. Here he was, sitting down with some of the very people he had refused to meet before the steel strike. (Besides Samuel Gompers, the Labor group included the heads of several unions belonging to the National Committee for Organizing Iron and Steel Workers.) Relishing the incongruity, Gompers rubbed in the irony of the situation. And Judge Gary, privately, registered his bitter resentment at "the uncalled-for personal remarks of the leader of the Union Labor Group.". Judge Gary had not originally been on the lists of nominees to the Public group, but when Baruch raised the idea of asking the unions to postpone strike action, the Judge's presence had seemed advisable. The invitation partially repaid Gary for denying the President's request to confer with the unions.[8]

Confronting the labor leaders was bad enough. At least, Gary felt, he was attending the Conference not as an employer but in the happier role of public representative.

Then, as he settled down to the ordeal, Judge Gary saw the steel strike brought squarely into the proceedings. When the strike resolution first came up for a vote on October 14, it faced almost certain defeat. But the Labor group, by quick maneuvering, secured a postponement of the vote pending a decision on the collective-bargaining resolution. "A movement to unionize the entire steel industry, by a few men . . . has developed into a strike managed in large part by the mover [Gompers] of the [strike] resolution," Gary complained to President Wilson in a letter he did not send. "Without [any] previous notice to me a resolution has been introduced . . . calling for an endorsement of a plan to settle the strike by arbitration. This resolution is undisposed of and hanging over the Conference for future consideration, notwithstanding the protest of myself and others."[9]

Immediately after the setback on the strike resolution, Judge Gary left the Conference for New York City to confer with his colleagues in the steel corporation. Everyone there agreed on the main points: that the strike "has no place whatever in the Conference's deliberation"; that, by considering the issue, "the Conference has exceeded the limits of its announced purpose"; and that, in any case, "this strike, so far as the United States Steel Corporation is concerned, cannot be arbitrated or compromised." Gary considered resigning from the Conference or boycotting its deliberations until the disposition of the objectionable strike resolution (both drastic alternatives were actually incorporated into draft letters to the President).[10] In the end, calmer counsels prevailed.

Judge Gary rejoined the Conference at the Monday afternoon session, October 20. Rumor had it that he carried a proposal which would break the stalemate. Gary immediately dashed such hopes. He recited routinely his belief in the open shop, in industrial efficiency and individual opportunity, in the generous treatment of labor, and "in conciliation, co-operation, and arbitration whenever practicable without sacrificing principle." Midway through came the key statement:

I am of the fixed opinion that the pending strike against the steel industry of this country should not be arbitrated or compromised, nor any action taken by the conference which bears upon that subject.

Judge Gary made no threats; he merely wanted the Conference to understand his position and his vote. That was enough. The Conference had no power whatever to require arbitration, and, since its main purpose was to find a common ground for labor and capital, no inclination to antagonize the mighty steel industry and its supporters. The Labor group instantly saw the point of Gary's speech. Unable to restrain himself, Gompers claimed the floor to express, emotionally and bitterly, his disappointment.[11] From that moment, no direct intercession in the steel strike could be expected from the Industrial Conference.

The other cause for hope remained. Union recognition was the central issue in the steel controversy. If the Industrial Conference adopted the main points of the Labor group's resolution on collective bargaining, the steel industry would face heavy public pressure to negotiate with union representatives. Everyone at the Conference agreed on the general propositions that men should have the right to organize and engage in collective bargaining. But opinion diverged widely on how to define and apply those principles. Agreement was hindered also by the voting procedure. The adoption of resolutions required a majority within each of the three groups. It was a situation made for a deadlock.

The Public and Labor groups came within inches of agreement. They differed on only two points. The Public representatives favored a definition of labor organization not limited to the trade-union form, and they wanted a guarantee of "the right of any wage earner to refrain from joining any organization or to deal directly with his employer if he so chooses." The open shop, one Public member noted, was "one of the hardest things for the labor men to take." But the Labor group, having consistently denied Gary's claim that union recognition would automatically create the closed shop, was willing to swallow the open-shop guarantee in exchange for this statement:

> The right of wage earners to organize in trade and labor unions, to bargain collectively, to be represented by representatives of their own choosing in negotiations and adjustments with employers, and in respect to wages, hours of labor, and relations and conditions of employment, is recognized.

A Labor and Public accord, on this basis, was presented to the full Conference on October 16, but two days later it came unstuck. After an ardent speech for "democracy in industry" by John D. Rockefeller, Jr., Public spokesmen again raised the issue of labor representation other than through trade unions. Then labor men blundered grievously. AFL Secretary Frank Morrison asserted that the resolution meant *only* trade unions. Further discussion revealed that one of twelve demands of the steel unions was elimination of company unions. Gompers, absent from the meeting with illness, later tried to put together the pieces. He repudiated Morrison's interpretation of the collective-bargaining resolution; he even gave assurances that, if U. S. Steel would confer with the unions, they would drop the company-union demand. But, by a margin of one vote, the Public members refused to support the original resolution. They insisted that "associations of their own choosing" be substituted for "trade and labor unions" or, as a concession, that "and other associations" be added to the latter phrase. The Labor group could not accept either of these apparent endorsements of company unionism.[12]

The Employer group had meanwhile developed an even harder line. They now demanded not only the open shop and a broad definition of labor organization but also "the right of the employer to deal or not to deal with men or groups of men who are not his employees and chosen by and from among them." The Labor group exploded over this last point. "There is the kernel of the objection," asserted Matthew Woll of the AFL. "Yes, we have the right to organize, we have the right to collective bargaining, oh, but we . . . have not the right to choose any other than those who are in employment with the employer with whom we are to deal. If . . . the right of selecting our representatives is to be limited in that fashion, then I say it is not a right, but it is an expression of servitude."[13] What value had the other rights if employers refused—as the steel industry was doing at that very moment—to deal with union representatives?

On Tuesday, October 21, the Industrial Conference voted on three collective-bargaining resolutions, one from each group. No proposal won the approval of any but its sponsor. (The steel-strike resolution was also formally defeated at this point.) Two weeks of debate and desperate bargaining had yielded a deadlock. That night the AFL Executive Council, which had earlier postponed action, decided to put its financial and moral support fully behind the steel strike.[14]

During his western tour the previous month, Woodrow Wilson had broken down under the strain and, after returning to Washington, suffered a stroke on October 2. Now, as Wilson's experiment with industrial peace neared a collapse, Chairman Franklin Lane appealed to the sick President to rescue the Conference. Over the objections of his physician Admiral Grayson, Wilson dictated a letter containing most of Lane's suggestions, penciled his signature with a shaky hand, and handed it to Joe Tumulty to deliver to Lane. The morning after the collective-bargaining impasse, Lane read the President's plea to the Conference.

At a time when the nations of the world are endeavoring to find a way of avoiding international war, are we to confess that there is no method to be found for carrying on industry except in the spirit and with the very method of war? Must suspicion and hatred and force rule us in civil life? Are our industrial leaders and our industrial workers to live together without faith in each other, constantly struggling for advantage over each other, doing naught but what is compelled?

My friends, this would be an intolerable outlook . . . an invitation to national disaster. From such a possibility my mind turns away, for my confidence is abiding that in this land we have learned how to accept the general judgment upon matters that affect the public weal.

But what was the "general judgment" on the main points of disagreement? Wilson gave no hint. Instead, he suggested that the collective-bargaining tangle be set aside, and the Industrial Conference address itself to "the development of that full program touching the many questions within the broad scope of your investigations."[15] This assuredly did not answer the needs of Labor representatives preoccupied with the crisis in steel. They had been on the verge of withdrawing from the Conference. Now, moved by the President's appeal, Gompers called his Labor group into caucus. The group came up with a final compromise proposal:

The right of wage earners to organize without discrimination, to bargain collectively, to be represented by representatives of their own choosing in negotiations and adjustments with employers in respect to wages, hours of labor, and relations and conditions of employment, is recognized.[16]

By setting aside the definition of labor organization, the Labor group hoped to win agreement on the free choice of representatives. The concession satisfied the Public group, but not the Employer group.

The head of the National Industrial Conference Board, Frederick P. Fish, immediately rose to protest. The earlier resolutions, he rapped out, had been designed to unionize American industry. "Now, they produce this resolution, which as a matter of words does not go as far as that; but words do not count. It is the thought behind the words; and . . . this resolution . . . would go out to the world as a concession on the part of the employers' group that they recognize the necessity of the unionization of all the industrial establishments in the country." Fish opposed the resolution "unless there is a plain definition as to what is meant by bargaining collectively, and the reservation . . . that the employers . . . shall not be required and forced against their will to deal with men . . . not of the number of their own employees. For that particular substantial issue cannot be evaded by any form of words." The steel strike had come instantly to Fish's mind. "We cannot read this resolution without reference to the history of the last two weeks and the events of yesterday. This matter of collective bargaining was interjected into the affairs of this conference to take the place of the resolution as to the arbitration of the steel strike with a purpose, and that purpose has clouded the conference from that time to this."[17] Conference and steel strike were deadlocked on an identical point: the employers' refusal to deal with outside representatives of the workers.

This admission, however, Judge Gary was reluctant to make. He far preferred to explain his company's stand as a defense of the open shop against unscrupulous labor leaders. He carefully avoided associating himself with the Employer group's position on union recognition, remained discreetly silent during the collective-bargaining debate, and abstained from the Public group balloting on the resolutions. As it happened, Judge Gary had been exposed even before the Conference.

The Senate Committee on Education and Labor had started an investigation of the steel strike. Judge Gary was among the early witnesses. For the most part, he received the deference befitting his high station, but a few Senators had asked him searching questions.

SENATOR THOMAS J. WALSH: Do I correctly understand your position to be this: First, will you admit you declined to see these men? Second, that you did not decline because of their official capacity, but because from your investigations, and inquiries, and your sources of information, you believed your workmen were contented and satisfied?

MR. GARY. You have given part of the reason, but not all.

SENATOR WALSH. Did you decline because they were officials of organized labor or because you believed they did not represent the true feelings and sentiments of your employees?

MR. GARY. That is right—that they did not . . . represent the sentiment of the large majority of our people, if any of them. Otherwise, we would have heard them, and of course if anything had been wrong we would have corrected it, as we always did. . . . We have made it our business to treat our men right.

. . . .

SENATOR WALSH. Was there any other reason for your refusal to hear these men, to see whether they did represent your men or not, except that your personal investigation satisfied you that they could not enlighten you any about the conditions of your workmen and their relationship to your company?

MR. GARY. Well, I want to be frank enough to say that it has been my policy, and the policy of our corporation, not to deal with union labor leaders.

SENATOR WALSH. Any way, at any time?

MR. GARY. At any time. And for the reason we do not believe in contracting with unions. When an employer contracts with the union labor leaders he immediately drives all of his employes into the unions. Otherwise, they cannot get employment. That is a part of the reason for trying to organize the men, and that is why we have been such an obstruction. I am not antagonizing unions, I am not saying that they have not a perfect right to form unions, of course they have; but we are not obliged to contract with them if we do not choose to do so. . . .

SENATOR WALSH. Is it not practically setting up an opposition to unions to refuse to meet and talk over labor conditions with their representatives? . . . Yet you say that the men have a right to unionize.

MR. GARY. Of course they have.

SENATOR WALSH. What good is the right to unionizing if the leaders or representatives can not talk with their employers? . . . Is it simply a social society?

MR. GARY. I do not think the leader[s] should undertake to talk with the employers—of a few of the men in the shop—when they know in advance that no contracts are made with the union labor leaders, and especially when the men themselves are not requesting it. . . . If a committee from any particular department, any one of them, desire to confer . . . they are welcome, regardless of the question as to whether they belong to unions or not. But in this case the union leaders were men entirely outside. . . . They had nothing whatever to do with our business or our affairs, any more than a man would have to interfere with the ——

SENATOR WALSH (*interrupting*). But, Judge Gary, if they had nothing to do with your business or with your affairs, how could they have gotten the men to follow them? . . .

MR. GARY. I will try to answer that, Senator.

SENATOR WALSH. If you please.

MR. GARY. I think about 10 per cent, possibly 15 per cent, have joined the union after a long campaign, and very many influences were resorted to in order to get them to sign up. But they called out all the employees. That was a part of the plan to organize the mills, which they had not been able to do otherwise. . . . When they went out and began their intimidation and all that sort of thing, a large number of other men stayed away, remained at home. That was part of the plan.

. . . .

SENATOR WILLIAM E. BORAH. . . . If these men, to use a slang expression, butted into this controversy and did not represent the employees . . . you were under no obligation in the world to see them; but it seems to me, underlying that proposition, that would be a mere fact of this particular controversy . . . is the other ques-

[125]

tion, as to whether or not great industries are willing to recognize
the representatives of unionized labor, and to deal with them.

MR. GARY. Senator, I think I should like to answer that question
in just this way. We are not willing to do anything which we believe, after consideration, amounts to the establishment of a closed
shop as against an open shop, or that tends to do that. We stand
firmly on the proposition, that industry must be allowed to proceed
untrammeled by the dictates of labor unions or anyone else except
the employer and the employees and the Government. That is
where we stand.

SENATOR BORAH. That is really the issue, as you conceive it to be,
in this controversy?

MR. GARY. It is.[18]

To anyone who cared to follow him closely, Judge Gary
thus revealed the real purpose of the open shop. The conclusion struck even the conservatives. Gary's testimony,
said the Springfield *Republican*, "puts beyond dispute his
opposition to unionism both in principle and practice."
"The reason he refused to confer with the organized labor
men," added the Brooklyn *Citizen*, "was because he is
opposed to organized labor."[19] Despite his evasions, Judge
Gary was, like the Employer group, clearly committed to
the defense of the employer's right—irrespective of his
men's desires—not to deal with union representatives.

The Industrial Conference ground to a bitter end. Late
in the afternoon of October 22, the three groups caucused
separately to vote on the final proposal of Labor. The
Public group favored it, but not the Employer group,
which meant, under the rules of the Conference, the
defeat of the resolution. Gompers rose to deliver his "swan
song." The Labor group had more than fulfilled its responsibility to find a common ground at the Conference. It
had accepted the open shop; it had retreated from its
insistence that trade unions must be the exclusive form
of labor organization; but it could not surrender on the
issue of union recognition. "You have by your action, the

action of the employers' group, legislated us out of this conference," Gompers concluded. "We have nothing further to submit. . . . We were endeavoring by all within our power to comply with the request made by that great man, now stricken on a bed of illness, the President of the United States, for whom we have an admiration and a love inexpressible . . . but we can no longer remain with you."[20] The AFL members filed out of the hall, and the next day the Conference adjourned.

The outcome seemed to justify the pessimism of some labor leaders. John L. Lewis of the Miners and Frank Duffy of the Carpenters, both refusing to attend, had doubted that "much good, if any [could] come from the conference." Now, as they had forecast, labor would have to continue the fight for its rights, as before, on the economic battlefield. The challenge had been thrown down, asserted Gompers, and labor could give "but one answer. The fight must go on. The weapons must be determined by the character of the struggle." From John Fitzpatrick came the brave words that the collapse of the Industrial Conference "strengthens the steel strike and means a fight to the finish with 'Garyism.' "[21]

Yet the contemporary judgment was misplaced. The Conference really amounted to a triumph for the union insistence on labor's rights. "The Conference did not," Bernard Baruch emphasized to President Wilson, "at any time, reject the principle of the right of workers to organize and bargain collectively with their employers. Neither the Conference as a whole, nor any one group in the Conference, opposed that right." Gompers's final proposal had received nearly unanimous support from the Public group, and lost in the Employer group by a margin of only 10 to 7. In the preceding debate, several employers in the Public group assailed the intransigent Employer group.

Its stand was patently unpopular. Baruch summarized the Public sentiment afterward for the President.

> We believe that the right of workers to organize for the purpose of collective bargaining with their employers, *through representatives of their own choosing*, cannot be denied or assailed. As representatives of the public we can interpret this right only in the sense that wage earners must be free to choose what organizations or associations, if any, they will join for this purpose.
>
> In the recognition of the right of workers so organized to be represented by representatives of their own choice, difficulties will from time to time arise. We believe that it would be possible for *a properly constituted arbitral authority to adjust such difficulties* with justice and fairness to all parties.[22]

Thus was the ground being prepared for the Wagner Act of 1935. But this fact gave the steelworkers cold comfort in 1919. They had hoped that the Industrial Conference would rescue their strike. There was an irony here: but for the tensions created by the steel strike, both Franklin Lane and Bernard Baruch felt, the Conference would not have deadlocked. Yet this was not the vital point. Even in disagreement, the Conference had revealed the swelling support for the union claim for recognition. Judge Gary was vulnerable, and he knew it. During his testimony before the Senate committee, he conceded that he might have met with union leaders had he received guarantees that they intended to speak only for the unionized employees, that they would permit others to make separate arrangements with the company, and that they would honor the open shop. Divided though it was, the Industrial Conference might well have generated massive pressure for collective bargaining in the steel industry. That this failed to happen was due to simultaneous events of another kind.

How did the country perceive the steel strike? "It is industrial war," thundered the New York *Times*. ". . . The

leaders are radicals, social and industrial revolution-
aries."[23] The New York *Tribune* considered it "another
experiment in the way of Bolshevizing American industry.
Its motive is political; its leaders have mobilized industrial
alienism for a disruptive purpose; and its purpose is un-
American." The strike, added the liberal New York *World*
during the first week, "has already taken on some of the
aspects of an economic revolution. . . . Even if the strike
is not primarily a *Soviet* raid against the steel industry,
it presents many of the indications of such a raid." The
Chicago *Tribune* did not doubt that "the decision means
a choice between the American system and the Russian—
individual liberty or the dictatorship of the proletariat."[24]

"It was the misfortune of the steel strike to occur in the
midst of the post-war reaction," William Z. Foster la-
mented afterward. The war had generated one-hundred-
per-cent Americanism and numbing fears of subversion.
Far from abating after the Armistice, the hysteria was fed
by all manner of events—the Bolshevik triumph in Russia,
unheard-of industrial conflicts such as the Seattle general
strike and the Boston police strike, the bomb outrages and
May Day rioting, and reports of secret Communist organizations poised for the revolution. Strike activity assumed
extraordinary proportions. One out of every five employed
workers was involved in a strike during 1919, a record that
has never been surpassed, or even approached, in American history. Not least, there were the politicians, journalists
and businessmen who, cynically or credulously, exploited
the terror gripping the country. By the time the steel strike
broke, men were ready to believe anything. "There is
hardly a respectable citizen of my acquaintance who does
not believe that we are on the verge of armed conflict in
this country," a West Virginia businessman confided to
Attorney-General A. Mitchell Palmer in October 1919.[25]

The steel strike fed such fears. Union spokesmen, of

course, insisted that the strike was an entirely conservative affair—called according to standard trade-union procedure, controlled by the vested authorities within the AFL, and aimed at the normal objective of union recognition and the improvement of wages, hours and conditions. All this was true, but there was more to be said. Union officials were, in private moments, awed by the magnitude and force of the walkout; it exceeded anything in the experience of the professionals. "The Iron and Steel strike is startling in the extreme," the former AFL treasurer John B. Lennon confessed to the chief U. S. conciliator on September 26. "All union men of Cleveland and nearby cities and towns are anxious to strike in sympathy. . . . The hopefulness of the union people is wonderful, if the fight be won great organization will follow, if it be lost danger of a most serious character threatens. The future is full of promise for the promotion of very great good or equally great evil."[26]

So thinking, labor men magnified what might result from the strike. Some expectantly awaited great changes in the wake of postwar "reconstruction." The railroad brotherhoods and the United Mine Workers of America, for example, advocated nationalization of their industries. Progressive unionists likewise predicted big things from the steel strike. "We are going to socialize the basic industries of the United States," proclaimed John Fitzpatrick in an incautious moment. "This is the beginning of the fight. We are going to have representatives on the board of directors of the Steel Corporation. President Wilson has promised that, in effect, in his program for the placing of industry on a better basis."[27]

Conservative unionists, for their part, drew equally extreme conclusions from opposite premises. Consider Gompers's plea to his antagonists at the Industrial Conference:

I say to you, gentlemen, you may win this steel strike unless you consent that it shall be adjusted after the fashion that we have so liberally proposed; but if you reject that method, and the steel strike . . . drags out, and you have won, and [the I.W.W., the Bolshevists of America] are going about the country and preaching the doctrine of their unbearable conditions . . . then, whatever betide, you have sown the seed and will bear the consequence. Our movement is constructive in character. You may dislike it. . . . You may not want to enter into agreements with us; but let me say this to you: You will either come to agreement with us or you will destroy the ability of the men in our movement to stand up for the right. We will be discarded as impotent or unfaithful; and . . . you will have somebody to deal with, and you will not find them arguing and appealing to you.

"The admission of Mr. Gompers himself that he is fighting bolshevism . . . bid us beware," Joe Tumulty remarked while warning Robert Lansing about the dangers besetting the country.[28] So, inadvertently, labor leaders who had every reason not to do so linked the steelworkers with radicalism.

From the Federal penitentiary in Atlanta, the Socialist Eugene Debs gave his first interview since being jailed for violation of the Espionage Act. The steel strike was, he said, "the old bitter contest that has been waged between capital and labor since time immemorial. And while I know the leaders of the strike do not counsel violence I am aware of the tactics that have always been adopted by the big steel companies. . . . I fear much violence will result from the strike." The prodigious struggle probably would draw in others "before it is over, and while I do not believe that a prearranged general strike will be called, yet . . . in the heat of passion men may lay down their work and be swept into a revolution with cyclonic fury." Debs concluded ominously: "Anything is possible as an outcome of the present situation."[29]

If the steel strike seemed so extraordinary to its leaders

and sympathizers, it could only appear terrifying to conservatives. They quickly found the marks of a radical conspiracy. Eastern European immigrants dominated the striking ranks. Even union leaders admitted that the aliens responded better to the organizing drive and the strike call than did the English-speaking workingmen. This was a point that the industry magnates eagerly hammered on. U. S. Steel sent a group of American steelworkers—skilled and highly paid men all—to Washington where they told the Senate investigating committee that they were well satisfied with working conditions, that they had no idea why the immigrants were striking, and that they had not even been invited to join the unions. Speaking for his own plant, the Homestead superintendent concluded "that possibly all of the Slovaks are out on strike, and that this is a Slovak strike." The steel corporation's general counsel pointedly asked the Senators: "Is it of account to know that in the investigation before you that these men have been able to come in and organize only the foreign element? Does that not bear on the general question?"[30]

It did indeed. The Eastern Europeans, wrote the New York *Journal of Commerce*, "have failed to become Americanized in character or sentiment." They not only "scoff[ed] at American ideals and institutions," but now threatened them. "The foreign element among the steelworkers," warned the New York *Times*, was "steeped in the doctrines of the class struggle and social overthrow, ignorant and easily misled." A popular poem by Edgar Guest, published in a steel-plant magazine, neatly drove home the point:

> Said Dan McGann to a foreign man who worked at the selfsame bench.
> "Let me tell you this," and for emphasis, he flourished a monkey wrench,

> "Don't talk to me of this bourjoissee, don't open your mouth
>   to speak
> "Of your socialists or your anarchists, don't mention the
>   bolshevik,
> "For I've had enough of this foreign stuff, I'm sick as a
>   man can be
> "Of the speech of hate, and I'm telling you straight, that
>   this is the land for me."

The strikers, a steel-town paper asserted, were "ignorant foreigners unable to understand the truth and blessed only with the belief that in some magical way they are to be put in possession of the mills."[31]

The existence of a Bolshevik conspiracy followed naturally from this image of the strikers. Press accounts pictured the steel districts in the throes of revolution. These were typical headlines from Pittsburgh newspapers:

1 SHOT, 20 HURT IN BRADDOCK STRIKE RIOTS, MANY HURT IN CLASHES BETWEEN STATE POLICE AND FORMER MILL WORKERS
(*Gazette-Times*, October 22)

DONORA RADICALS TRY TO BLOW UP HOME AND BRIDGE
(*Press*, November 11)

DONORA AND ENVIRONS TERRIFIED BY BOMBS—REIGN OF TERROR EXISTS FOLLOWING DYNAMITING OF HOMES AND STREET CAR—FOUR ARRESTED ON 12-YEAR-OLD BOY'S TESTIMONY   (*Sun*, November 7)

STEELWORKER'S HOME BOMBED AT DONORA: FOUR ARRESTED
(*Press*, November 30)

When investigators from the Interchurch World Movement checked these stories, they found them to be either false, misleading or unrelated to the strike.[32] Actually, the strike was remarkably peaceful; what violence there was stemmed mainly from the repressive measures of the police. But the truth was less consequential than the popular belief that murder and mayhem gripped the steel districts.

Meanwhile, an assiduous search began for the radical conspirators behind the strike. At its start, the New York *Times* reported that in the Chicago district Federal agents "stepped in with the avowed purpose of suppressing radical agitators, lest the strike be used as a means of advancing Bolshevism." The Department of Justice, already scouring the country for radicals, now concentrated on the strike centers. Hundreds of steelworkers were detained, most of them aliens who could be deported as undesirables. From Sharon, Pennsylvania, came the account of a wild gun battle between state constabulary and a den of IWWs and Bolsheviki. Three blocks of entrenched Reds were cleaned up, a small arsenal of weapons confiscated, 75 men arrested and six killed, chiefly snipers on rooftops. That the story lacked corroboration, and that the New York *Times* reported its source as U. S. Steel channels, probably did not lessen the shock effect.[33]

The Red hunt soon focused on Gary, Indiana. There rioting broke out against strikebreakers on October 4. Two days later, as the trouble intensified, Federal troops arrived on the scene. General Leonard Wood, commander of the Central Military District at Chicago, enthusiastically shared the spirit of the Red scare. The country, he confided to U. S. Steel's George W. Perkins, had to "make a much more serious and thorough effort to Americanize the immigrant who comes to us" and "of promptly getting rid of the alien or naturalized Red, either by deportation or proper legal procedure."

The destructive group is small but well organized. . . . We must impress upon all these people—and our own who have become disaffected—that true liberty is found within the law and never outside it.

General Wood (who had Presidential aspirations) naturally construed his duty not only to quell the Gary disorders but also to do "my part in the rounding up of the Red element."[34] As soon as the military forces moved in, the search commenced. Newspapers featured stories of "wholesale seizures of firearms, radical literature and red flags." An intelligence officer spent an entire day before the Senate investigating committee describing the evidence of radicalism in Gary—caches of weapons, secret societies, bundles of IWW and Communist literature, foreigners professing a belief in violence and revolution.

What did this have to do with the steel strike? The young intelligence officer revealed the connection inadvertently before the Senate committee:

SENATOR McKELLAR. Are there many Russian workers in and around here?

LIEUT. DONALD C. VAN BUREN. In my opinion they predominate.

. . . .

SENATOR McKELLAR. About what proportion of the Gary workers out on strike would you say are foreigners?

LIEUT. VAN BUREN. Oh, a large majority are foreigners. In my examination, sir, of these suspect radicals that have been brought to me or come to my attention, I have not seen a single American-born.

. . . .

LIEUT. VAN BUREN. But I would like to say . . . that all the laboring men of Gary that belonged to the American Federation of Labor are not reds by any means. There is a sprinkling of Americans in that group.

The lieutenant confidently equated radicals with aliens; it followed that the strike was a radical enterprise. But the Army claimed still more concrete proof of the conspiracy. "If the military department revealed the evidence it has gathered in Gary," commanding Colonel W. S. Mapes hinted darkly, "the strike would break at once." Such statements issued regularly from Gary military headquarters.

[135]

When union spokesmen protested, the Army either did not answer or pleaded misquotation. Lieutenant Van Buren patently failed to demonstrate to the Senate committee the tie between the radicals and the strike. In fact, no more could be shown than that a few of the alleged radicals were also strikers; no evidence ever revealed Bolshevik control of the strike in Gary. Even the charges of local radical activity were ludicrously exaggerated. It did not matter. Gary was proof, the Portland *Oregonian* insisted, "of an attempted revolution, not a strike."[35]

To clinch the case against the steel strike, a master conspirator had to be found. Here labor's opponents fell upon singular good fortune—they discovered William Z. Foster, the secretary of the National Committee for Organizing Iron and Steel Workers. Foster's radical past was well known among his union colleagues. Back in 1911, he had drawn the ire of the AFL when, as an IWW, he had tried to prevent the seating of the Federation delegate to a world labor conference in Budapest. Later, he broke with the IWW and became an organizer for the conservative Carmen's Union. Gompers came upon Foster at a meeting in Chicago, and was impressed by him and gratified by his support. The old man saw that Foster "could be of real service to the cause of labor. He was a man of ability, a man of good presence, gentle in expression. . . . I was willing to help build a golden bridge for mine enemy to pass over." Foster's role in the union drives in meat packing and now in steel seemingly justified Gompers's confidence. When a turncoat labor paper in Pittsburgh attacked him in the spring of 1919, Foster offered his resignation and received a vote of confidence from the National Committee.[36] After that, Foster's past was forgotten.

Then a reporter from *Iron Age*, nosing around Pittsburgh some days before the strike date, heard of Foster's earlier life and, what was worse, came across a pamphlet written by Foster some years before. *Syndicalism* was a violent tract, filled with denunciations of the capitalist order and extreme prescriptions for change—the work, as Gompers later ruefully remarked, of "a young man [who] dogmatically laid down the phantasies of his brain." On September 12, the journalist went to the National Committee headquarters in Pittsburgh, a couple of small rooms in the Magee Building. Presented with the reporter's information, Foster remarked softly that some was true, some not; as for his book, it had been written eight years before. "The important point is, not whether I have done this or that, in the past, but have I today the absolute confidence of Samuel Gompers? I say to you Gompers looks only to results. He knows me. He knows what I have accomplished. . . . He trusts me and that is enough." *Iron Age* next presented Gompers with a copy of Foster's pamphlet. The AFL chief of course brushed aside the suggestion that it was grounds for calling off the strike. In its issue of September 18, the magazine broke the story with these portentous words: "To permit the strikes of workers in the iron and steel mills . . . as proposed by a small band of agitators would be a crime against civilization."[37]

The headline flashed across the country as the walkout began: STEEL STRIKE LEADER IS CALLED ADVOCATE OF ANARCHIST IDEAS. The pamphlet, long out of print, appeared overnight in the steel districts. Newspapers printed long extracts from it as an integral aspect of their strike coverage.

If society is even to be perpetuated—to say nothing of being organized upon an equitable basis—the wages system must be abolished. The thieves at present in control of the industries must be stripped of their booty and so reorganized that every individual shall have free access to the social means of production. This social reorganization will be a revolution. Only after such a revolution will the great inequalities of modern society disappear.

. . . .

The syndicalist . . . considers the State a meddling capitalist institution. He resists its tyrannical interference in his affairs as much as possible, and proposes to exclude it from the future society. He is a radical opponent of "law and order," as he knows that for his unions to be "legal" in their tactics would be for them to become impotent. He recognizes no rights of the capitalists to their property, and is going to strip them of it, law or no law.[38]

The author of these fiery words, men reflected, was now leading the steel strike! It was as much as many ever did learn about the great struggle.

On the second day of the strike, Congressman John G. Cooper of the steel-producing Mahoning district in Ohio claimed the floor in the House of Representatives. "I hold in my hand here a pamphlet entitled 'Syndicalism,'" he announced in the manner a Senator named Joseph Mc-Carthy would make famous three decades later. "I charge that Mr. Foster's own words in this book show his unfitness as a labor leader and disqualify him from the name of an American citizen or the protection of the American flag!" And then the peroration: "We all only have to recall what happened in Boston a few days ago [in the police strike] to know what always takes place when the forces of law and order give way. . . . Let those bloody agitators, anarchists, Bolshevists and syndicalists point to some other land which is freer and fairer than ours, and then if they find there is such a country let them rid us of their presence and retire to that utopia." The entire gallery and many on the floor of the House stood up and cheered. In Pittsburgh, Foster had no comment.[39]

The denunciations rose in pitch. The New York *Times* prayed that the misled steelworkers would recognize "the ulterior and actual designs of the radical and revolutionary agitators who have engineered this strike movement." In

Washington Julius Kahn, chairman of the House Military Affairs Committee, proposed an idea to Attorney General A. Mitchell Palmer. Would it not be possible to prosecute Foster as an accessory if it could be proved that strikers who committed murder and other crimes had been influenced by Foster's book? "Such theories as this man Foster has advocated are a menace to the country and make him a menace, too." And in Wilmington, Delaware, Judge Joseph Buffington of the U. S. Circuit Court of Appeals, presiding over naturalization proceedings, took it upon himself to denounce Foster as "a dangerous domestic enemy" and to warn the new citizens to beware of him and his kind.[40]

Labor leaders answered these attacks as best they could. Foster had long since dropped his radicalism; it had been a youthful aberration common enough among intelligent men of Foster's poverty-ridden background. Could anyone find a single remark during his tenure as secretary of the National Committee that showed he still held his earlier views? What was more, they added, Foster had no real power. He was merely a salaried functionary who followed orders. The authority rested with the National Committee. And no one could impugn the twenty-four constituent unions, or the AFL of which they were a part, with the charge of radicalism. Their only objective was "that the men in the steel plants of the United States shall enjoy what millions of workingmen outside the steel mills are enjoying."[41]

Yet it took but little ingenuity to build a case against Foster. Why, first of all, had he originally broken with the IWW? Not over ends, but over tactics. He had favored "boring from within" rather than revolutionary dual unionism. The Senate investigating committee made much of Foster's statement during his unsuccessful bid in 1911 for the editorship of the IWW organ, *Industrial Worker*.

The only way for the I.W.W. to have the workers adopt and practice the principles of revolutionary unionism . . . is to give up the attempt to create a new labor movement, turn itself into a propaganda league, get into the organized-labor movement, and by building up better fighting machines within the old unions than those possessed by our reactionary enemies, revolutionize these unions, even as our French syndicalist fellow workers have so successfully done with theirs.

Yours, for the revolution,
Wm. Z. Foster

If he advocated boring from within, would he not do exactly what he was now doing in the AFL? Foster's mild manner was deceptive. He was, wrote George Smart, "not vigorous physically and speaks usually in a low voice. He impresses one as being anything but a noisy agitator. . . . Foster is of a different type and to my mind is far more dangerous."[42] Nor was it accepted that, as secretary, Foster wielded little influence within the steel movement. He had introduced the original resolution at the AFL convention in 1918 and, it was generally known, taken credit for initiating the drive and getting it moving. In reality, Foster was, together with John Fitzpatrick, a key man in the National Committee and, in some ways, the brains of the outfit. It would have been closer to the mark to have acknowledged Foster's importance, but as an agent whose powers and policies depended on approval from the member national unions.

Radical control of the strike signified a power struggle within the AFL. Samuel Gompers was of course impeccably respectable. "No one ever imputes any question about your patriotism," a Senator assured him deferentially. "You did as much to win the war as anybody, and everybody knows it. But the American Federation of Labor, they say, is not squarely behind the strike, but that radicals like Foster . . . that class of men, radicals, who are against the institutions of our country, are using this . . . and getting into the American Federation of Labor and trying to control it in that way." This idea rested, as did others, on a certain factual base. Gompers had considered the strike ill-advised; he had urged postponement, and his advice had been disregarded. He was old and tired—more so, his most recent biographer has in fact noted, than the public realized. The New York *Tribune,* among others, reasoned that while Gompers was in Europe during the summer, the radicals had gained control and pushed the steel movement to a crisis. By September, conservative leaders "were obliged either to agree or step aside or stand the combined attack of the radical factions of the AFL, thus endangering their control of the organization." Gompers's defense of Foster, concluded steelman E. T. Weir, "shows that the old man has lost his grip and that the AFL is in the hands of the extremely radical element." So, through the single figure of Foster, men could reconcile the contradiction of a strike at once radical and AFL-supported. It could even be opposed, as the New York *Times* piously did, on the grounds that defeat would preserve conservative control of the AFL.[43]

On the afternoon of October 3, 1919, in a Washington room packed with reporters, William Z. Foster took his seat before the Senate committee investigating the steel strike. It was his opportunity to puncture the charges against him. After some preliminary testimony, the interrogation began. "Mr. Foster, are you in favor of organized Government?" Senator Kenneth McKellar of Tennessee broke in. "Mr. Chairman, I see the Senator is reading from the red book," retorted Foster. "Yes sir; and I want to read to you from it." Senator McKellar chose some flaming passages on "The Revolution." "Is that your honest belief now?" he asked. Foster hesitated. He wanted to be judged not by his private beliefs, he said, but by his words and acts as a trade-union functionary. Pressed by the Senators, Foster agreed to talk freely, but not before the biased press because "no matter what I say it will be misconstrued. It is bound to be misconstrued." In exasperation, Gompers, who was sitting close by, hissed at him: "They cannot say anything worse of you than they have said." Foster was willing to make "a repudiation of that pamphlet, as a whole, and a general statement that I do not subscribe to the doctrine in it." But on specific points, he continued to be evasive and vague. He would not say when he had changed his views: it was a matter of "historical growth." Questioned about some passages, he answered that he would not write them in the same way; about others, he said he only partly disagreed.[44] Gompers had not bargained for this. What the occasion required was abject renunciation, a confession of past errors, a ringing statement of faith in the standing order. As it was, Foster's testimony merely fed the fires.

What was Foster up to? No evidence exists that Foster was acting as the agent of a radical organization. The emerging Communist groups were disorganized and, as they themselves admitted, entirely unable to exploit the steel strike. Foster had not yet embraced communism. Nor was he a friend of the IWW. To that syndicalist organization, committed as it was to dual unionism, Foster had fallen into the fatal trap awaiting the borer-from-within: "Instead of becoming a leader in the movement, he becomes a follower . . . he must lose his identity, and . . . that is exactly what happened with Mr. Foster; he lost his identity." Actually, Foster had not betrayed his revolutionary goals. From their very nature, he argued, "the trade unions are making straight for the abolition of capitalism . . . incomparably faster . . . than any of the much advertised, so-called revolutionary unions. . . . Progressives must be won over from the idealistic and utopian to the evolutionary point of view. . . . The power

[142]

of even a few such men, proceeding intelligently along practical lines, is one of the marvels of the labor movement."[45]

This course, on which Foster was then embarked, bred its own problems. Could the progressives guide the trade unions without arousing the suspicions and then the opposition of the conservative leadership? Foster had succeeded so far, but the public attacks on him and his performance before the Senate committee made a difference. In his autobiography, Gompers claimed to have grown disillusioned with Foster at this time, and others had similar feelings. As far back as October 1918, the archconservative AFL organizer Emmet T. Flood had privately charged that the Chicago packinghouse drive was "controlled by Bolshevikis. . . . Some of these same people are now very active in the campaign of organization among the steelworkers." Federation officials began to watch Foster closely; indeed, to monitor his speeches secretly.[46] Foster's days within the AFL were numbered.

But, for the moment, there was nothing to be done. No purpose would be served by firing Foster. Trouble would surely follow inside the steel movement; for, whatever his private views, Foster had not acted at cross purposes to the AFL establishment. His services in the strike, moreover, were highly valued. "He talked a vigorous militant language, in the conventional terms of trade unionism," John Brophy recalled. "There was a minimum of flamboyance in his speaking. It was a pretty orderly mind . . . better than the general run of leaders in similar positions. . . . Foster could direct and administer far-flung organized effort, though with inadequate forces." Finally, his dismissal would only corroborate the charges against the strike; certainly it would not stop criticism.

The damage was already done. The last piece had been fitted in place to complete the picture of the steel strike as a dangerous radical movement. The National Committee admitted the fact privately: "Because of the tremendous power and influence of . . . the United States Steel Corporation . . . the men in active charge of the strike have been thoroughly discredited."[47]

The radical issue quashed the strikers' main hope for a settlement. Public intervention was ruled out. The steel industry found in the radical conspiracy justification for a policy that was no longer defensible as a general proposition. John J. Raskob made the point at the President's Industrial Conference. The Labor group maintained that an employer should deal with any representatives chosen by workingmen, irrespective of the former's character. Therefore, Judge Gary should accept Foster and his like. But surely the public would "not insist that he must deal with representatives, or claimed-to-be representatives . . . who are I.W.W. men and so on. I think public opinion, in that case, is strongly in favor of Judge Gary." As Raskob saw it, the question was "whether the employers shall have the right [not] to deal with representatives who are not within their own plants, if the moral situation justifies them in so refusing." That was precisely how steelmen wanted the issue posed. No patriotic American, however favorably disposed toward labor's right to organize and engage in collective bargaining, could condemn U. S. Steel for refusing to deal with Reds. So reasoning, the New York *Times* opposed any attempt by the Industrial Conference to bring the two sides to the bargaining table: it would strengthen "the radical leaders of the steel strike, men who believe in the socialization of industry, in taking the factories out of the hands of their owners and putting them into the control of the men employed." Judge Gary himself brusquely dismissed a mediation offer by prominent churchmen because the strike's intent was "the

[144]

closed shop, Soviets, and the forcible distribution of property."[48]

As it stiffened industry resistance, the radical issue sapped the Federal Government of any sympathy for the steelworkers' cause. Labor leaders had expected, on the basis of wartime experience and President Wilson's stand before the strike, that help would be forthcoming from Washington. They were quickly disabused of that hope. Certain key men in the Administration were themselves victims of the Red scare. Joe Tumulty, for example, found "abundant evidence on every side that propaganda is afoot to advance the Soviet idea and to weaken the morale of our people, especially in labor circles. I do not think we gain anything by temporizing with it."[49] Even the calmer heads could sense clearly enough the popular sentiment setting in against the steel strike. President Wilson, incapacitated by a stroke, provided no brake on the smaller men in his Administration. When strike leaders complained of terrorism and the suppression of civil liberties, they received no help from Washington. Attorney General Palmer remarked that "it is beyond the jurisdiction of the Department of Justice to interfere in purely local affairs." Attempts to secure mediation were handled with similar coldness. Secretary of Labor William B. Wilson, up to this time an AFL partisan, rejected out of hand the suggestion that the War Labor Board be reactivated to consider the steel strike. The summary memorandum in the files of the Department of Labor read:

Pursuant to the policy of the Department not to intervene in any labor dispute unless and until either the employers or employees or the public directly interested requested its good offices, the strike was not at any time brought within the jurisdiction of the Department.

The conclusion was accurate, if not the explanation. Disillusioned strikers decided "that the corporate interests are in the saddle politically, that they dominate every department of the government." "We have found out what to expect from President Wilson and the mangy administration," rapped out one angry organizer.[50]

The steel strike as a public event bore no fruit for labor's cause, or, more precisely, bore bitter fruit. Hysteria licensed the repressive measures of the steel interests and their local allies, and even enlisted some governmental aid on management's behalf. Finally, the radical issue divided and confused the steelworkers. The unions' private war with the steelmakers was rendered so much the harder by the failure of the public phase of the steel strike.

5

The Steel Strike: Private War

THE GREAT STEEL strike pivoted on external events, on the response of public opinion and political authority. Waged on a grand scale in America's steel centers, the strike itself really was in the nature of an historical detail. For, once public intervention was ruled out, the outcome became a foregone conclusion.

A week before the strike, John D. Rockefeller, Jr., had called on Henry Clay Frick, still a major figure in the counsels of U. S. Steel. "I found him utterly opposed to collective bargaining and representation," Rockefeller told his industrial-relations adviser, W. L. Mackensie King, "and ready to close up every mill if a strike occurred. He believes that this is the only course and is prepared to follow it at any cost."[1] The steel strikers, for their part, could not hope to exert sufficient economic pressure to break down such determination to preserve the open shop and the prerogatives of management. Strengthened by five years of abnormally high incomes, the powerful steel industry could have withstood even a total shutdown, and unionists never expected the strike to be total. Assessing the prospects beforehand, Samuel Gompers had pressed for postponement. Business unionist that he was, Gompers valued strikes only as an economic weapon that gave reasonable promise of success. And here, the old man knew, there was no such likelihood.

Once the issue was joined, it remained only to be seen how the steelmakers would proceed to crush the strike.

[147]

On Sunday afternoon, September 21, several thousand steelworkers, many with their families, filled an open field in North Clairton, fifteen miles up the Monongahela River from Pittsburgh. These employees of U. S. Steel's Clairton Works, a union strongpoint, had gathered to receive instructions for the strike scheduled for the next morning. The crowd, very quiet, was listening attentively to the second speaker. Hearing a sudden commotion, P. H. Brogan, the local union chief, looked up to see half a dozen high-helmeted state police bearing down on the speakers' stand at a gallop. "They rode right in where the meeting was, it was packed with men, women and children. These constables were using their big long clubs, striking the people on both sides of their horses, cursing and swearing." One trooper reached the front of the platform and, unable to drive his horse up onto it, tore down the American flag. Amid plunging horses and the screams of women and children, the crowd scattered. Some men turned to pick up stones. Brogan mounted the platform and shouted at them: "Go home, go home or you will get shot." One trooper did empty his revolver, evidently for effect; no one was hit. A number of men, Brogan among them, were taken to the Clairton jail, held overnight without food, driven to Pittsburgh the next morning and booked for disorderly conduct. It was the beginning of the terror in the Pittsburgh district.[2]

The day before the Clairton incident, Allegheny County had issued an emergency proclamation directing all peace officers to prevent the congregation of three or more people in any outdoor public place. Sheriff William S. Haddock explained that the prohibition would prevent "the customary troubles of an ugly strike. . . . The agitators are very active and stage every incident they can, such as . . . meetings when permitted, etc., to attract the workingman's attention." Indoor meetings were permitted at the discretion of local authority, so long as they were conducted in English. "This is America," Sheriff Haddock later remarked, and "my observation has been . . . that practically 90 per cent of the offenders against the law in matters of this kind are either aliens or naturalized citizens of foreign extraction, who are easily led into attacks upon our Government."[3] The leeway left by the sheriff hardly benefited the strikers. The steel towns utilized their local ordinances to restrict or entirely prohibit indoor meetings. In McKeesport, the local unions could not even hold business sessions, much less strikers' rallies. Pittsburgh itself permitted meetings only at two halls some distance from the strike zones. The gains of the free-speech campaign in the district, painfully won a short time before, were now ruthlessly swept away.

Before the strike came, the steel companies asked Sheriff Haddock to create a body of deputy sheriffs to handle the trouble everyone anticipated. The request was customary in such circumstances, and the sheriff was happy to oblige. He deputized some 5,000 men, selected, paid and armed by the steel companies. The measure, he assured the Senate investigating committee, was no expense at all to the county. For their part, the employers thus had disposal of a large contingent of local citizens and loyal workers, clothed with the authority of law, presumably to keep order, prevent the intimidation of nonunion men, and protect company property. The state constabulary also arrived on the scene. The troopers actually numbered no more than 50 in the entire county, spread thinly among the important steel towns. But the "Cossacks" (so called by the strikers) made up in effectiveness what they lacked in numbers. Highly trained in riot tactics, impressively uniformed and mounted, they struck fear among the strikers and provided the cutting edge of the police authority.

The Clairton incident revealed how the forces of law and order would be used in western Pennsylvania. "Last week the cossacks were very busy in the mornings beating our pickets and taking them to jail," a Monessen striker reported. From another steel town came this telegram to the Labor Department: "Reign of terror in Newcastle, caused by deputies in uniform of soldiers. Women and children arrested for nothing. Send investigator." And, laconically, from Donora: "The state police keep everyone moving or club them down."⁴

The administration of justice, no less than the keeping of the peace, was made to serve partisan purposes. The Interchurch World Movement discovered the widespread use of such practices as the following:

. . . the arresting and holding of men and women for long periods in the jails and police stations without provocation, and even without definite charges being lodged against them; the excessive punishment meted out to these strikers by the different Justices of the Peace, Burgesses and Police Courts, and the frank discrimination in the courts between those who were at work and those who were out on strike. . . .

Here is how, in one among uncounted similar incidents, the terror touched a dozen immigrant steelworkers on a Monessen street early on the morning of October 8:

JOHN YILLAWICH. I go myself. State constable came and put me in a bunch. . . . Three State constables come from this way [*indicating*] and some run away and some club. One fellow fall on the sidewalk. . . . He will kill himself, the constable said. . . . He put us in the tube mill gate, and it was dark and no lights on it. . . . They opened the door and opened the light, too, and put us down in the cellar. No. 1 State policeman go around and ask how old and American citizen and anything, and always ask us. Well them fellows go away. The other fellow said—he stood on the other side —he said, "You fellows are going to be hung about 8 o'clock."
GEORGE WAKALE. Some guys come over there, down to the cellar, you know, and tell the fellows, he said, "If you go to work, everything is all right; if you don't, you have to go to jail."

John Yillawich. Well, for 7 o'clock come, come a patrol wagon, takes down to jail. Well, I sit in jail until half past 4 after dinner, and my wife come three times that day down there. She said, "John, you go out," she says. "Well, I want to go out; need a $500 bail. . . ." She go around and get one fellow—he got his property, you know—and sign his name and take me off for $500 bail.[5]

The strikers learned the meaning of law and order, western-Pennsylvania style.

The strike situation encouraged the harsh policies of the local authorities in the Pittsburgh district. Elsewhere, the walkout tended to be total; in western Pennsylvania, it was only partial. And here the strike divided on ethnic lines. The strikers were mostly unskilled immigrants, the very element held suspect by the local middle class. "The population of the town is approximately 85 per cent foreign, and a large number of such foreigners are of the radical—so-called Bolshevik—element," the Donora burgess explained in his plea for state troopers. Violence seemed inevitable: part of the labor force was at work, and the rest were dangerous foreigners. The crisis called for repressive measures. Men could claim, as did the president of the Monessen town council and leader of the vigilante Citizens' Protective League, that "we were entirely disinterested, and formed the committee only to preserve order in the town."

The Pittsburgh district actually remained relatively peaceful. A wild riot did break out in Farrell. For one tense moment in Monessen, armed citizens led by state troopers confronted a large parade of strikers coming from Donora. But, in the end, everyone agreed that order had prevailed. "Allegheny County has had no real violence," Sheriff Haddock acknowledged. "We attribute this entirely to the earnest co-operation of all peace officers from the policemen to the mayors."[6] To Pittsburgh authorities, the bloodless character of the strike signified the success, not a refutation, of the tough policy.

Nor did repression hold political risks. When united, steelworkers were politically potent. Even in western Pennsylvania, local officials showed restraint where the strike was strong—for example, in Johnstown. Although his town was created and economically dominated by U. S. Steel, the mayor of Gary, Indiana, honestly pursued a neutral line, and reluctantly called for military intercession only at the actual outbreak of rioting. The Cleveland mayor sided openly with the unions, and prevented strikebreakers from entering the city until stayed by court action. In Lackawanna, New York, a steel center adjacent to Buffalo, the labor organizations joined in the mayoralty campaign and helped to defeat the incumbent. As the AFL organizer on the scene reported, "Immediately we could feel and see the stock of the steel strike rise. . . . The new Mayor, knowing that the steel strike and those engaged therein were responsible for his success, declared in favor of the strike. . . . Free speech would be permitted and public gatherings would be encouraged, and everybody, especially the steel strikers, would be given a fair and square deal."[7] The steelworkers could hardly respond so effectively in western Pennsylvania. Not only were they divided, but nonstriking Americans spoke for the blue-collar constituency. No political liability—just the reverse, in fact—attached to fighting the strike in the Pittsburgh district.

"The strike situation is not a waiting proposition for us," remarked a Carnegie Steel official in western Pennsylvania. "We are running our big mills. It is the strikers who are doing the waiting. If these plants can continue to run, without molestation, those who are striking will soon be back." The strategy was simple and certain: protect those who would work, cow the others, isolate them and ultimately drive them back into the mills. Strikebreaking in turn depended, as a Carnegie executive noted, on "the protection afforded by the State Constabulary and the local officials." This was "generally good, but where it failed the strike has made headway." Another Pittsburgh steelman added that "the continued good order has helped us materially, because, with the fear and intimidation removed, many workmen have returned." He was also candidly pleased by measures that "reduced strike propaganda to the minimum." An identical assessment came from desperate strike leaders. Foster pleaded for some action by the AFL to halt the suppression of civil liberties in western Pennsylvania. "Unless this course can be checked very shortly and these indispensable rights re-established in these important districts the favorable outcome of the strike will be greatly endangered, if not entirely destroyed."[8] Both sides understood the efficacy of the police power in the Pittsburgh situation.

Little could be done. Recourse to the courts, as anticipated, failed to halt the repression. Attempts to generate a public outcry likewise fell short. Foster urged Gompers to invite a committee of "public-spirited men" to visit the strike zone. "Of course time would be a great factor in the value of the work of this committee, the need for relief being most urgent."[9] Pittsburgh labor leaders journeyed to Washington to petition the Congressmen from the area. The Pennsylvania Federation of Labor held a special conference in Pittsburgh on November 1, and threatened to call a general strike in the state as a protest. A priest in Braddock, Father Adelbert Kazincy, incensed to see his parishioners set upon by the state constabulary as they left his church, objected loudly and drew some attention. It was all to no avail. Pennsylvania Governor W. C. Sproul demanded proof of the charges against his state police, and then ignored the bundle of affidavits subsequently sent to him. The Senate investigating committee heard testimony and received affidavits from the victims of repression in the Pittsburgh district. Yet the evidence made little impression, bemused as the Senators and the press were with the danger of radicalism. (The investigating committee's presence did, however, temporarily reduce police activities in the district.) The sheriff of Allegheny County denied any interference with free speech or free assembly, with the noteworthy afterthought, "except in strike zones by local officers, or by the sheriff for extraordinary reasons."[10]

If labor leaders had anticipated help from Washington, the Federal Government demolished that hope by its actions at the one point where it took a direct hand in the strike. Soon after entering Gary, Indiana, the Army stirred up accusations of unreasonable restriction on strike activities and intimidation of strikers. On October 10, Chicago district leaders sent an angry telegram to Washington charging "steel trust partisanship . . . by War and Justice Department officials." Attorney General Palmer curtly dismissed the complaints after receiving routine assurances from his agents at the scene. Secretary of War Newton D. Baker was more disturbed:

The function of the War Department in this instance is to assist the Governor [of Indiana] at his request, in the maintenance of civil order. Neither the War Department nor the soldiers under its direction have any right to take sides in a labor dispute. . . .

"Any such action would be so entirely improper," Baker said, that he was directing General Wood to make a thorough inquiry.[11] The general, however, had his own ideas about the responsibilities of the military. No relief was granted, and, next only to the Pittsburgh district, Gary suffered most grievously from hostile men vested with public authority.

Steelmen were satisfied. "If the Monongahela plants succeed in operating non-union, the other plants will have to operate non-union or not at all," said one confident Carnegie official. "The strikers have to get the Pittsburgh district or they are through." Throwing all available organizers into the district, the National Committee could not break the grip of repression.

The strike never actually collapsed in western Pennsylvania. During the first week, foremen and superintendents visited strikers' homes, and full-page advertisements appeared in all the local papers: GO BACK TO WORK MONDAY. To the visible surprise of many observers, the anticipated break failed to materialize on that morning, September 29. Nor did it occur later. Foster, in fact, believed the harsh methods toughened the resistance of the hard core of strikers in the district. Still, the Pittsburgh situation answered the purposes of the steelmakers. Production dropped sharply in the first week, but then rose gradually until by the end of November it approached normal.[12] Since the Pittsburgh district produced a quarter of the country's steel, and operations also remained high in the South and East, steelmen could afford to wait out the strike at its strongpoints.

To begin with, enthusiasm ran remarkably high among the strikers. They had demanded the walkout, and they would fight hard. The industry had a stubborn battle on its hands. For many steelworkers, the strike was a continuation of the wartime struggle for democracy. Judge Gary, proclaimed John Fitzpatrick, would be "the last of that line of tyrants who had been in a position to dominate the lives of the workers all these years." The caption under the photograph of a young steelworker killed during the strike underlined the main point:

Casimir Mazurek, who fought on foreign soil to make the world free for Democracy, was shot to death by the hirelings and thugs of the Lackawanna Steel Co. because he fearlessly stood for industrial Democracy on American soil.

The sense of grievance over the actual terms of employment was thereby intensified. One Amalgamated lodge petitioned the Secretary of Labor:

We struck because we knew that this action proved to the world that we were striving to bring into every household conditions that would perpetuate the best principles upon which our government was founded.

. . . .

Now that the war is over and the world made safe (?) for Democracy, what do the workers (the ones who sacrificed all) receive?

They are allowed under the new democracy to starve while the storage houses are overflowing with plenty; allowed to shiver with cold when there is wool and cotton in abundance; allowed to walk the railroad ties in search of work when plants are idle for lack of men. Is this the democracy we won in the late war?

The strike, as a Cleveland man saw it, had a clear purpose: "We are going to finish up in this country [the struggle for] democracy, a living wage and the right to organize."[13]

Men were so deeply committed, Foster remarked after the failure of the employers' first back-to-work campaign in the Pittsburgh district, that "the only way to beat them is to starve them out." This was not easily accomplished in 1919. Most steelworkers had worked steadily for four years. The war had enforced savings in the Liberty Loans, and the immigrants tended to save in any case. (This fact partly explained the difference in the relative sticking power of the foreign-born and English-speaking men during the strike.) The National Committee devised an effective method of assistance as the strike entered its second month. The normal form of aid—weekly cash benefits—was precluded by the extensiveness of the strike, and only two of the lesser craft unions provided such payments to their striking members. Instead, the National Committee set up a Commissariat to distribute food packages to needy strikers. A fund-raising drive collected $418,000—$150,000 from a rally in Madison Square Garden on November 8, and most of the remainder from unions without any direct interest in steel. Imaginatively conceived, efficiently administered, and adequately financed, the Commissariat served its purpose: no one starved during the steel strike. Discussing the resources of his men, one plant superintendent grumbled: "They can stand it for three years."[14]

The tenacity of the immigrants was a special source of strength. "When they strike," wrote an observer who had worked in the steel mills, "they strike until the day of settlement. Others may take their places or they may go to work elsewhere, but they won't sneak in through the back gate." Labor leaders seemed surprised; they had doubted the mettle of the immigrants. The error only revealed the persistence of stereotypes of the foreigner. Immigrant workmen had repeatedly showed in steel mills, in coal mines, and elsewhere, their toughness in industrial warfare. Strikes had the force of a communal action among immigrants. In Pueblo and elsewhere wives joined their men on the picket line. To violate the community will peculiarly disturbed the immigrant, for he identified himself, not primarily as an individual in the American manner, but as a member of a group. "Slavish" strikers in Monessen wanted to return to work, a company spy reported, but were "holding back for no other reason than that they would be called scabs and have a bad name among their fellow employees after the strike would be over." Observers noted that nonstriking immigrants were either outcasts or men expecting to return to Europe. The wartime ideology, moreover, especially infused the immigrants. "For why this war? For why we buy Liberty Bonds?" asked a Polish striker. "For mills? No, for freedom and America—for everybody. No more [work like] horse and wagon. For eight-hour day." The immigrants, concluded the National Committee, "are proving to have wonderful powers of resistance."[15]

On the other hand, strong immigrant support also created liabilities for the strike movement. A ready weapon was at hand to split the "Americans" from the larger body. The English-speaking men and the foreigners would have been hard to unite at any time. Now the currents of the Red scare swept through the industrial districts. A nativist appeal deliberately exploited the resulting social tensions in the mill towns. At International Harvester's Wisconsin Steel Works, the superintendent urged the employee representatives, as "good red-blooded Americans," to vote in favor of reopening the plant after the second week of the strike. The issue, insisted the *Gary Works Circle*, was "Americanism vs. Bolshevism." An advertisement appeared in the Pittsburgh *Gazette-Times*:

AMERICA IS CALLING YOU

This is no ordinary strike. Rather it must be looked upon as the diabolical attempt of a small group of radicals to disorganize labor and plant revolution in this country. . . . Keep America busy, and prosperous, and American. Go back to work.

In Gary, Indiana, businessmen reactivated the Loyal American League, a wartime vigilante agency, to protect the mill city during the strike. The league devoted itself primarily to financing warnings in the local press against "the parasite with nothing to lose except the other fellow's belongings and with everything to gain . . . whether you call him Bolsheviki, IWW, Agitator or Enemy." "There is such a thing as Americanism, and it is involved, it seems, in this strike."[16]

The charge surely hit home. In Gary, 117 striking skilled steelworkers called reporters into a meeting. Highly paid men, enemies of extremism, and citizens all, they wanted to "refute the idea printed in the papers that the steel strike is being led and directed by the radicals in the labor movement and that only the foreigners want this strike. . . . We expect to continue until we win, but at no time do we intend to resort to any violence or other methods that would discredit us in the eyes of the Constitution." One striker reviled the claim that a man cannot be "a loyal American unless he is a scab . . . unless you give up all the rights your country gives you and obey your employer."

The unceasing attacks on strike leaders likewise had an impact. Even the skeptics, as testimony before the Senate investigating committee revealed, were hard put to refute the charges against Foster. An organizer wrote in despair:

> You may be right, but you will not find a hearing; your position may be perfectly in harmony with the fundamental law of the country, the industrial autocrat will shout you down. . . . So long as you have not the power to enforce your thoughts you are like one crying in the wilderness.

In the end, many strikers surely returned to work because they "called themselves good loyal Americans."[17]

The strikers' morale meanwhile came under quiet attack from a hidden source. The steel companies invested heavily in labor espionage. One Monessen independent, evidently considering its practice to be normal and expected, permitted Interchurch Movement investigators to inspect its "labor file." The papers turned out to include 600 reports from undercover agents. Even Judge Gary, on being asked whether U. S. Steel had an espionage organization, murmured that, although he could not be specific, he was "quite sure that at times some of our people have used secret-service men to ascertain facts and conditions. That is intended to be at least a frank answer, and perhaps it is over-frank." The Corporations Auxiliary Company, a leader in the field, claimed to have 500 operatives active in the steel strike.

Defeatism was the chief objective. For example, Agent Z-16, sent by Corporations Auxiliary to Monessen, intended "to become acquainted very rapidly with the different elements and factions here and believe I shall be able to influence a good many men to return to work." His reports reveal his methods:

> I took occasion to take all four of these men to a cafe, bought them a drink and we left in time to see the men leaving the plant after stopping work for the day. When my companions saw the men file past coming from work they became very envious and jealous and one of the group was prompt to say:
> "I don't care what happens, I am going to work tomorrow."
> "If you do I'll do so myself for I am in pretty poor shape financially and have a family of my own to support," I stated.
>
> .   .   .   .
>
> The meeting tomorrow afternoon at Charleroi undoubtedly will have considerable effect on the attitude of the men [whom he thought were wavering], and I shall carefully watch and take opportunity to seize upon every opening that may be given me to continue propagating along these lines and today I really feel as if we shall see a serious break in the ranks . . . very shortly.

The agents of defeat reached into the union officialdom in Pittsburgh and Wheeling and (if a Pittsburgh detective agency chief is to be believed) even into the National Committee itself.[18]

Confidence could be poisoned openly as well. How was the strike going? Men found out mainly from their newspapers. The prohibition of meetings made the printed word the only regular source of strike news in the Pittsburgh district. And strike coverage in the local press was sweeping in its bias. "A reader of the Pittsburgh newspapers from September 22 to October 10," observed a journalist investigating the matter for the Interchurch World Movement, "must have gained the impression that the large number of men conceded to have gone out on September 22 had done so with no other intention than that of turning round and flocking back to their jobs beginning September 23." The *Gazette-Times* ran banner headlines on the second and third days of the strike:

SITUATION IMPROVING, CARNEGIE STEEL
CO. ASSERTS: MILLS HERE RUNNING

Night Shifts Go Back To Work,
Few Men Held Back By Fear

MORE MEN RETURN TO MILLS

Carnegie Steel Plants Report Men Returning	21,000 Said to Have Gone Back to Work ——— Several Plants Closed Monday Reopened

Such accounts piled up until, as one sardonic observer figured it, forty-eight times as many men had reported for work as there were jobs in the district.[19]

The situation varied away from Pittsburgh. In the commercial centers of the Youngstown, Cleveland, and Chicago districts, certain major papers—for example, the Cleveland *Plain Dealer*—gave fair accounts of the progress of the strike. In the mill towns, where the newspapers were tied into the power structure of local business and mill management, the strike reporting was no better than in Pittsburgh. "Our own newspapers will make it appear that the mills are running with full crews," one local correspondent warned. ". . . That is not true. . . . Lebanon is still on strike." The Cambria Works at Johnstown had been closed tight for eight weeks when the Midvale management announced the resumption of operations on November 17. The next day, the Johnstown *Leader* proclaimed: THE STRIKE IS BROKEN. As it happened, an Interchurch World Movement man was on the scene. He drew a different conclusion from personal observation: the company had attracted only a tenth of the normal work

[161]

force and had failed to make a successful start. The Johnstown strikers discovered readily enough the truth about their own situation; they derided the plant whistle at the shift changes as "the call of the last hope." But about the strike elsewhere they were, as one of them complained, "up against it for news."

The National Committee strained its resources to make itself heard. A professional publicity man was hired, bulletins were distributed to the strikers, meetings were scheduled more frequently. The strikers were warned: "The public press is against us." But, in the end, the National Committee acknowledged its failure to counteract the "subtle, undermining effect . . . [of] 'enemy propaganda,' used with every facility to make it effective."[20]

At the end of October, the industry moved to the offensive. Strikebreakers arrived on the scene. Steel companies recruited widely, but concentrated on Negroes. Since 1915, large numbers of black migrants had moved into the mills. Except in a few places, such as Cleveland and Wheeling, they had proved almost immune to the union appeal. In the great mills of the Pittsburgh district, a mere handful out of the thousands of Negro steelworkers joined the strike. Others still on the outside now signed on as strikebreakers. For them the strike meant an opportunity to find a place in American industry. Theirs was not the union cause, community leaders and steel companies told them. Many labor organizations, including some involved in the steel drive, excluded or segregated Negroes. Exploiting the racial situation, the industry drew Negro strikebreakers from the large Northern cities and even from the South. Afterward, the National Committee estimated that over 30,000 Negroes had entered the industry during the strike.

This number—roughly a tenth of the total body of strikers—revealed the limited aims of the steelmen. At first underestimating the importance of the Negroes, strike leaders soon saw the accuracy of the industry's stroke. The strikebreakers served the psychological purpose of undermining the faltering strike ranks. Reporting Chicago conditions, a union official warned of the "bad effect on morale of the white men to see blacks crowding into the mills to take their jobs."[21]

The other aim was, of course, to produce steel. By themselves, the inexperienced Negroes could do little of that. But, as it happened, their rough labor met the industry's needs, for the skilled men almost everywhere proved the weak link among the strikers. Some, unwilling to scab on their friends, found jobs in struck plants in other centers. Then, as the union lines began to crack visibly, the key skilled men led the return to work. Secretary Foster admitted that the high-paid men "showed little tenacity as strikers. . . . When the strike came, the unskilled workers led the way . . . with the aristocratic steelworkers bringing up the rear. But in scurrying back to scab in the mills, the order was just the reverse." Now, too, the employee representation plans proved useful vehicles for the back-to-work movements. At the Wisconsin Steel Company, the works council received the tasks of voting the company's decision to reopen the plant and then of screening the returning strikers. So, as November advanced, production began to rise in plants hitherto closed tight. The Chicago District Council had to inform the National Committee on November 21 of a "situation beyond control, with a possibility of holding the organizations if they are shortly released from the strike order."[22] The strike elsewhere, while not so desperate, was clearly deteriorating.

The pressure rose another notch. Local business and public men nearly everywhere had favored the management side from the start. But, outside the Pittsburgh district, union strength had discouraged interference. Now, as the labor ranks weakened and businessmen's impatience mounted, antistrike measures began to take form elsewhere. In Youngstown a petition, originating among local merchants and circulated in mid-November, complained of the unendurable situation and expressed opposition to "the Bolsheviks or any other malcontents, whose movements may lead to industrial turmoil." The municipal council president demanded that William Z. Foster be notified to keep away or at least make his stays in Youngstown as short as possible. Men talked—nothing more—of driving the local strike leaders out of town. On November 22, the district secretary and two organizers were arrested and charged with criminal syndicalism. And finally meetings were prohibited. An entire local union of 71 men was arrested for holding a business session in East Youngstown.

Danger signs appeared elsewhere. The Donora *Evening Herald* warned darkly that organizers "are no longer wanted in this community." In Johnstown a mob led by the chamber of commerce president and the YMCA secretary forced Foster and four organizers to quit the city in early November. "Unable otherwise to break 100 per cent solidarity of the 20,000 Johnstown Steel Strikers," Foster wired Gompers, "Co. has frankly embarked upon policy of violence. Beginning by deporting organizers. I went last night. . . . Can you . . . halt this outrage."[23] Gompers could not. But the gust of terrorism subsided, and the organizers (not including Foster) returned to Johnstown. A second attempt at mob action failed to drive them out at the end of November. A month later, an unknown assailant shot at the steel-plant superintendent in Pueblo, Colorado, providing the occasion for calling in state militia and prohibiting picketing. These late actions served not so much to impede the strike as to set the seal of hopelessness on the strikers' cause: every man's hand was against them.

Strikers were simultaneously discovering the feebleness at the heart of the union movement. Two lines of authority actually existed. One line ran to the twenty-four national unions with jurisdiction in the steel industry. Theirs was the highest power. They alone decided the extent of their contribution to the joint effort, and they were the only judges of their own actions. The key question was whether the national unions would subordinate their authority to the other line of command—the National Committee for Organizing Iron and Steel Workers. The National Committee acted merely as a voluntary body, an agent of the twenty-four autonomous nationals. "It is not bound together by any constitution or law or anything, except just common interest," Secretary Foster explained. But the National Committee alone could unite the efforts of the national unions. The emergency forced an expansion of its authority. The Machinists' representative on the National Committee, William Hannon, noted the fact.

> This steel strike was handled differently from any strike that I have ever been connected with. In practically every other strike . . . the officers of the International organizations affected have handled the situation, acting as an executive committee to direct the strike. In this strike, the Secretary of the National Committee assumed the leadership, the International representatives having but little to say about its direction. Of course, when the National Committee met, the action taken was generally approved . . .

The national unions, although they could not be required to do so, also tended to accept majority decisions in the Committee. They acquiesced, Hannon grumbled, "in the interest of harmony. . . . We raised no protest, because a protest at that time would have created dissension, and dissension is bad for the strikers, if it exists among the officers in charge."[24] Through the vehicle of the National Committee, the strike enlarged the unity of action and diminished the accustomed particularism of the national unions.

But the crisis also had an opposite effect. Each union's leaders had to weigh the interests of their own organization against the claims of the steel strike. Initially, such calculation, based on misplaced pessimism, had so limited the first investment as to waste the wartime opportunity. Now defeatism again narrowed the commitment of the national unions. A few, excited by the immensity of the conflict and the significance of the issue, contributed beyond their measure. Others, sure of the final result, looked only to their own interests.

None was more culpable in this respect than the Amalgamated Association of Iron, Steel and Tin Workers. This was the pivotal union, encompassing, as it did, all the jobs specific to steelmaking. The union was torn between the old and new. The Amalgamated had long since shrunk to a minor organization of skilled workmen in a few finishing branches of the industry, and was strongly oriented toward exclusiveness, the status quo, and business unionism. (Its constitution required that "Every member shall interest himself, individually and collectively, in protecting his trade, and the business of all employers who recognize, negotiate and are under contract with this association.") During the war, the Amalgamated had begun to exercise its large, residual jurisdiction in steel, and thereby gradually became liberalized. Its journal claimed in May 1919 that "the transition of organization from a straight out-and-out craft organization to a live industrial organization has been successfully effected." But the top leaders—men like garrulous, kindly President Michael Tighe—were of the old school. They identified themselves with the skilled base of the prewar years, and not with the new organizations that had suddenly sprung up. Caution now proved a powerful imperative, for the Amalgamated had everything at stake. As the basic organization in the industry, Tighe argued, "Its very life depended on maintaining that position; if it lost that, it had no other to fall back on. All the other[s] . . . had their basic organization outside of the iron and steel mills."[25]

The strike immediately raised an issue touching that vital point. Amalgamated contracts covered roughly 5,000 skilled men in a large number of independent finishing mills. The unskilled men in those plants, now members of the Amalgamated, remained as yet outside the contracts, but one curious clause affected them:

> Should the employees of any departments (who do not come under the above-named scales or contracts) become members of the Amalgamated Association during the said scale year, the Amalgamated Association may present a scale of wages covering said employees, but in case men and management can not come to an agreement on said scale, same shall be held over until the next general or local conference, and all men shall continue work until the expiration of the scale year.

"That was put in there for the purpose of protecting our contract," explained the president of the Wheeling Steel and Iron Company. "It was known that other people might come in during the year to go into the association."[26] Blinded by its concern for the skilled men, the Amalgamated had blundered into a trap. The contract would be violated if men not parties to it went on strike to win its benefits.

The men did strike, and many of the contract men came along in sympathy. The union took the position, as its representative repeatedly told the National Committee, "that contracts are sacred to the Amalgamated and will be lived up to under all circumstances." More than the principle was involved. Employers warned that they would consider the entire contract abrogated if the one clause was violated. The Amalgamated faced the loss of its secure base if it did not comply. Acquiescence, on the other hand, would grievously hurt the general strike, especially in the Youngstown and Wheeling districts. Was the contractual obligation to employers more sacred than the moral responsibility to the other unions? John Fitzpatrick asked. The Amalgamated of course also owed an obligation to itself. Tighe saw but one course. He ordered the men back to work. Recalcitrant lodges, as in Cleveland, lost their charters.

The decision ripped the fragile unity of the union enterprise. Within the National Committee, biting criticism met the Amalgamated. In the field, strike leaders demanded that the order be ignored. Anyone who returned, Youngstown district secretary J. E. McCadden announced, would be a scab. Afterward, Tighe expressed to Gompers his resentment against the Committee's "Secretaries and Organizers trying to invade our mills where we had contracts signed and which would have destroyed our organization if they had been allowed to have their way. The situation became very unpleasant to us." As for his critics, Tighe told them in effect to mind their own business. To do otherwise, he grandiloquently scolded an offending Bricklayers' official, would be "gross discourtesy and can only be attributed to ill-breeding or consummate ignorance. For no true trade unionist would be guilty of traducing another organization" which had not "in any manner interfered with the workings of his organization."[27] As an autonomous union, the Amalgamated was answerable to no one for its actions. That was the sad truth of the matter. The National Committee could only be as strong as the sum of its member unions.

The union-mill issue hardly tested the Amalgamated fairly. No union could be expected to commit suicide in any cause, however supreme. But other evidences of Amalgamated weakness were abundant. For one thing, the union took away far more than it gave to the steel drive. Half the recruits went to the Amalgamated, each bringing two dollars in initiation fees and dues as long as he remained a member. Despite the resulting income, the Amalgamated contributed only grudgingly to the movement. When the call went out for additional organizers for the embattled Pittsburgh strikers, the Amalgamated sent not one. It expended less than half of a special strike fund raised from a 2 per cent levy on its membership. Far from sacrificing for the steel drive, the Amalgamated benefited handsomely from it: cash reserves nearly tripled between 1918 and 1920. Moreover, the union had some slight success in making separate deals to lengthen its list of sheet and tin mills. Finally, the Amalgamated quickly lost heart in the fight. It was one of two unions (the other, the Operating Engineers, was openly fighting the National Committee and was about to be expelled) to vote to end the strike on December 14. Pessimism infected its organizers and, especially in the Wheeling district, undermined the striking ranks.

What had happened was clear enough. After a brief fling at expansiveness, the Amalgamated was retreating back to past ways. Explaining his differences with the National Committee, Tighe revealingly remarked that "we did not claim jurisdiction over the lodges who had requested to take a strike vote; we only claimed those lodges where we had contracts."[28] In the end, he eagerly sacrificed the former—indeed, exploited them—for the sake of the established skilled men's organization.

Other unions were equally remiss in their support. Only $46,000 was actually forthcoming for the strike fund of $100,000. Several other unions were guilty of defeatism and of failing to pull their men out during the strike. Jurisdictional squabbling made a strange spectacle in the National Committee at a time when the strike itself was collapsing. H. M. Comerford of the Operating Engineers —disgruntled, among other reasons, because the Electrical

Workers had been granted the cranemen—publicly blamed John Fitzpatrick in early December for mishandling the strike. All of this revealed the difficulty of focusing the policies and resources of autonomous unions, each with its own interests, on the unionization of a new area. The expectation of defeat cast a pervading gloom; the scent of victory might have elicited a quite different response. As matters stood, in any case, no action by the unions—the Amalgamated included—would have reversed the decline of the strike.

Only one kind of move might have served. The steel companies were vulnerable to attacks on the flow of materials to and from the mills. Many Great Lakes seamen had struck in sympathy with the steelworkers, impeding the shipment of ore from the Minnesota ranges. But the timing of the strike had offset the effect of this move. Ore reserves at the mills, geared to the freezing of the Lakes in winter, neared their peak in September. The national coal strike seemed to hold greater promise. In fact, according to *Iron Age*, Pittsburgh steelmen believed (erroneously) that the coal strike "was partly brought about and largely influenced by the leaders of the steel strike, who hoped that cutting off coal supply and closing the mills might bolster up the steel strike."[29] But the anticipated impact proved inconsequential. The steel strike was six weeks old and faltering when the United Mine Workers went out on November 1; the companies had large coal stocks on hand; and then the Federal Government intervened and secured an injunction against the miners. If anything, the steel strike was actually harmed. On the one hand, the coal dispute prevented the Mine Workers from contributing financially to the steel strike. On the other, it revealed with stark clarity the political forces that were setting in against labor's cause.

One final stroke, more modest in its dimensions, might

have pinched off the vital arteries of the steel industry. Short switching lines connected the steel mills to the main railroads. If such links as the Union Railroad and the McKeesport and Monongahela Railroad were cut, the balance would swing in the critical area of the strike. The Pittsburgh district would be silenced, increasing the strike's economic impact on the industry immensely. National Committee investigators found that the Pittsburgh connecting lines were owned by the steel companies, that the railroaders were mostly organized but without contracts, and that they were inclined to join the strike if given some direction. At a conference in Washington, the National Committee urged the railroad brotherhoods to take strike votes among these men. The brotherhoods, true to their long history of particularism, proved uncooperative. In the case of the important Trainmen, the coolness derived also from a jurisdictional clash with the AFL's Switchmen's Union, a member of the National Committee. Since no contracts would be violated, however, the brotherhoods permitted their members to strike on their own initiative. In Youngstown the railroaders did come out, but not in Pittsburgh. The Brotherhood of Railroad Trainmen finally ordered a strike vote there, but the critical period had already passed. A strategic blow, whose consequences might have been large, was thus sadly dissipated.

The strike meanwhile was deteriorating rapidly. Following reports of a sharp break the previous week, the National Committee analyzed the situation for twelve hours on Monday, November 24. The unanimous decision was to hold on. After adjournment, however, several leading members began to discuss among themselves how the strike might be settled. They were certain that they themselves could not do it; the industry simply would not

[171]

deal with them. Some outside agency had to be brought in. The logical choice, the Federal Government, had ruled itself out after the failure of the Industrial Conference.

This left the influential Interchurch World Movement. Recently founded to represent American Protestantism in secular affairs, the Interchurch Movement was already studying the steel strike through a Commission of Inquiry. The directing churchmen, Bishop Francis J. McConnell and Dr. Daniel A. Poling, had given the National Committee reason to be confident of their sympathy and fairness.

On November 27, John Fitzpatrick went to New York to seek the Commission's good offices to end the strike. The next day, the Commission agreed, but set two conditions. It would act independently, not as a representative of the unions, and it would follow its own ambitious plan:

1. To mediate in behalf of all the steelworkers, both those still on strike and those who had gone back to work.
2. The purpose of mediation should be to establish a new deal in the steel industry rather than merely end the strike.
3. The ending of the strike should be arranged solely with a view to giving the new deal the best possible chance.

In accepting the proposal on December 1, the National Committee stated explicitly that the Commission was free to set aside "our old original demands as a basis of negotiation, [and] to start anew with whatever requirements they feel justice demands." If the steel industry accepted the churchmen's intercession and agreed to abide by their recommendations, the National Committee would order the men back to work and then, as the Commission understood it, "step out of the situation."* To the Commission,

---

* The agreement between Fitzpatrick and the Commission was actually somewhat shaky. According to Fitzpatrick's account to the National Committee, the strike would end only after the steel industry accepted arbitration by the Commission. The Commission, on the other hand, spoke only of mediation toward a "new deal"; it did not say that its recom-

these seemed "extraordinary concessions," and "any reasons advocated by the employers for not accepting the mediation plan would have to be weighty."

Bishop McConnell, Dr. Poling and Dr. John McDowell thereupon secured an appointment with Judge Gary for Friday morning, December 5. It was a remarkable meeting. Judge Gary produced an "anonymous" report accusing the Interchurch Movement of being infiltrated by "red radicals." Before he would discuss anything else, the Judge minutely examined the distinguished clerics about these charges. (They were actually prepared, since the report had dogged the efforts of the Commission of Inquiry for several weeks; one of the clergymen, in fact, took a copy from his pocket when a secretary brought in Gary's own.) Having disposed of this nonsense, the ministers started to explain their mediating mission. They did not progress far. Judge Gary immediately took charge of the interview. He expounded at length his philosophy of welfare capitalism; he insisted the strike was radical in intent, that the men at work were content and that those still out were "nothing but a group of red radicals whom we don't want anyhow." The churchmen tried to pin Gary down but, as they remarked ruefully afterward, "it was rather difficult to ask questions."

Courteous as always, Judge Gary was engaging in a shrewd maneuver. On the one hand, the Interchurch spokesmen were too important to dismiss. On the other hand, their proposals for a strike settlement could not be considered. So Judge Gary talked for two hours without permitting them even to present their "plan of mediation." (The plan would have involved "a permanent mediation

---

mendations would be binding on the industry. And Fitzpatrick did not tell the National Committee that its ties with the movement would be cut, only that the ending of the strike would be placed entirely in the hands of the Commission. As it happened, there was no occasion for reconciling these discrepancies.

body to bring about a conference between employers and employees in the steel industry.") As the interview closed, Dr. McDowell asked: "In your mind, then, Judge Gary, you consider that for you and the Steel Corporation there is no issue to be discussed?" And Gary's last word: "There is absolutely no issue." On departing, the Interchurch representatives decided against any public statement. What could they say?[30]

Somberly, the National Committee met in full session in Washington on December 13. Now no hope remained for a negotiated end to the strike; the industry wanted unconditional surrender. After detailing the district reports, Secretary Foster made this calculation: of the 365,500 originally claimed to be on strike, 109,300 still held out, and production ranged between 50 and 60 per cent of normal (a most conservative estimate). The delegates could not bring themselves to halt the fight. "This is a life and death struggle for unionism in the steel industry," one man had said at the previous meeting. ". . . If we should give up now, it would mean the destruction of our organizations. The only thing we can do in the situation is to fight to the last ditch." So the unions voted, fourteen to two, to continue the strike.

But the end was in sight. By January 1920 the strike remained effective only at scattered points. In the major districts—Chicago, Youngstown, Wheeling, Cleveland—the fight was lost. On January 8, the National Committee finally gave up. A telegram, defiant still, went out from union headquarters: "All steelworkers are now at liberty to return to work pending preparations for the next big organization movement."[31]

Afterward, strikers found little enough to show for the tremendous fight they had waged. "Mr. Gary may claim the material victory," wrote a Machinists' organizer assigned to the Chicago district, "but the moral victory rests with the unions." The brave words rang hollow in the mill towns. Steelworkers drifted back to their jobs embittered and apathetic. Some activists were weeded out in the rehiring process. On the whole, however, blacklisting occurred infrequently. The companies needed men, particularly after they let go the many poor workers among the strikebreakers. But in the mills the atmosphere remained apprehensive. "Men are [afraid] of the Petty Bosses," a Wheeling unionist complained to the Secretary of Labor. "The Prostitutes of manhood go to men and say Don't Belong to the union, Don't Pay Dues. . . . See, you did not win the Strike, the union is no good. They say this to Both ignorant Americans and Foreigners and scare them and they are [afraid] to attend meetings and to Pay [their] Dues." The strike, however, marked the men not so much with fear as with despair. During the summer of 1920, a team of interviewers circulated through the steel towns. They heard repeatedly that "it is useless to strike or fight the big companies. . . . The worker will have to bear it."[32] Neither the steelworkers nor the unions would soon be ready for a second round.

Despite its imperfections, the joint steel drive really marked a major advance in the labor movement's response to mass production. Some unionists immediately proposed a renewed effort that would profit from the mistakes of 1918–1919. But nothing of the sort happened. As soon as the strike was over, the Amalgamated resentfully withdrew from the National Committee. Unable to function without this key union and unwilling to take the radical step of ignoring its jurisdictional rights, the National Committee disbanded on July 1, 1920. Thereafter, the Amalgamated insisted on a dominant voice in any subsequent drive. When William Z. Foster emerged as a leading American Communist, disillusionment deepened. Gompers publicly admitted he had been wrong about both Foster and the steel strike: "The movement was premature and . . . badly conducted." The second organizing campaign in steel was repeatedly postponed and then dropped entirely after an abortive attempt in the summer of 1923. Indifference, the official in charge glumly reported, was "not confined to the unorganized steel mill workers" but also was "manifested by officers and representatives of the several international organizations."[33]

Organizing resources meanwhile diminished. The Amalgamated Association, for one, found little return on its investment in good will. The industry applauded the union for honoring its contracts during the strike, but that praise did not prevent employers, when the occasion arose, from casting aside the Amalgamated. By 1929, its membership had fallen to the level of 1914. Other national unions with steel jurisdiction likewise were on the defensive. The 1918–1919 union effort could not be duplicated, much less improved upon, in the 1920's.

If organized labor failed to capitalize on the great strike, so did the steel industry. Bankrupt though its labor program demonstrably was, no new ideas emerged. Judge Gary was trapped in his own rhetoric. Until his death in 1927, he repeated the same worn phrases of his welfare philosophy: "Be unselfish, reasonable, fair, sincere, and honest . . . without interruption; give evidence of a disposition to conciliate and co-operate." As for U. S. Steel, "We have treated our men better than . . . any large industrial concern ever before treated its men in any country or in any period."[34] The steel strike revealed to Judge Gary, not a flaw in his own approach, but the irrationality of the workingman and the low cunning of union organizers.

The strike, in fact, set back the one new development in the industry's labor program. Employee representation had gained support among steelmen during the war. Judge Gary was not one of them, but he had wavered. Now he pointed to the Colorado Fuel and Iron Company's plan. It was the oldest and best developed in the industry, yet Pueblo had experienced a complete walkout. Proponents answered that the test was unfair. Still, employee representation made no converts after the great strike. At Bethlehem, the strike actually undermined the most independent of the representation plans. The shop committees lost their connection with outside unions and fell completely under the thumb of the company. No liberalizing influence informed the industry's labor policies after 1919.

Indirectly, one notable improvement did grow out of the strike. The Interchurch World Movement had conducted an independent investigation. When it appeared in summer of 1920, the report caused a sensation, for it refuted many distortions widely held about the great steel strike. But, as a call to action, the report misfired. It quickly became shrouded in the familiar controversy over radical influence in the investigation. The chief recommendation—that a Government commission establish a "conference" relationship in the industry—inspired no response from any quarter. (The Wilson Administration, when approached by Interchurch leaders before the release of the report, refused to touch the idea.)[35] One fact, however, instantly gripped public attention: steelworkers regularly worked twelve hours a day and many worked a seven-day week. That schedule seemed unconscionable in the New Era.

Immediately, pressure developed for a reduction of hours. Even within the industry, reform sentiment existed. Directly after the steel strike, U. S. Steel director George Perkins urged Judge Gary to act. "With the splendid record you have made before the country, the leadership in this matter clearly belongs to you and can be made of the greatest possible value in solving our present difficult problems."[36] Gary's earlier directive against the seven-day week, reversed by wartime needs and unco-operative executives, now received firmer enforcement. But the twelve-hour turn presented harder problems. Eight hours, the only alternative in continuous steel operation, would considerably increase both work force and labor costs. As in his consideration of the issue before the war, Gary was impressed by the objections of practical steelmen. He did start a study, but quietly shelved it during the depression of 1921.

Public opinion, however, would not be denied. In 1922, under the prodding of Secretary of Commerce Herbert Hoover, the White House itself interceded. The industry thereupon appointed a committee, presumably to come up with a plan. When Judge Gary, a full year later in May 1923, deferred any change, the outcry became irresistible. Nothing better revealed the general indignation than Rollin Kirby's cartoon of gaunt, weary men coming out of a steel mill and, underneath, Judge Gary's remark: "The workmen prefer the longer hours." The break finally came when President Harding, already entering the last sad days of his Administration, expressed keen disappointment to Judge Gary on June 18, 1923. The following week the industry pledged to eliminate the twelve-hour day as soon as the labor supply permitted. By the end of the summer, the eight-hour day, plus a compensating wage-rate increase of 25 per cent, was largely in effect. As it turned out, neither the dislocations nor the cost increases were as great as steelmen had persistently predicted.

So something of value did result from the great strike. But the eight-hour day, desirable as it was, was not the vital issue in 1919. The steelworkers had fought for collective bargaining through independent unions. That goal seemed far distant in the 1920's.

[178]

6

A New Beginning

LABOR failed to carry steel in 1919. The union movement had gathered unexpected momentum, struck the entire industry in September and, despite the immensity of the struggle, receded without victory. Labor's cause had broken before Judge Gary's uncompromising defense of the open shop. The defeat seemed irreversible. Yet Gary's legacy outlasted him by only a decade. In the 1930's, the Committee for Industrial Organization (CIO) began to take hold in steel. By the mid-1940's, the steel industry was thoroughly organized and fully engaged in collective bargaining. The disaster of 1919 had proved to be only a postponement, and not a final denial, of the benefits of unionism for America's steelworkers.

A chance encounter started the breach in the industry's wall of resistance. On January 9, 1937, Myron C. Taylor of U. S. Steel came upon CIO chief John L. Lewis in the dining room of the Mayflower Hotel in Washington. Casually, the two agreed to meet privately the following day. During the next seven weeks, the aristocratic millionaire and the hard-willed labor leader held a series of secret discussions. An unexpected personal affinity permitted the two commanding men to explore the explosive issue between them. On February 25, Taylor offered a formula:

The Company recognizes the right of its employees to bargain collectively through representatives freely chosen by them without dictation, coercion or intimidation in any form or from any source.

[179]

It will negotiate and contract with the representatives of any group of its employees so chosen and with any organization as the representative of its members, subject to the recognition of the principle that the right to work is not dependent on membership or non-membership in any organization and subject to the right of every employee freely to bargain in such manner and through such representatives, if any, as he chooses.[1]

Three days later, on a Sunday morning, John L. Lewis entered Myron Taylor's New York town house with his mind made up: he would accept the proposal.

STEEL BOWS TO LEWIS' UNION.[2] The momentous headline rocked the country, so perfect had been the secrecy of the Lewis-Taylor talks. On March 2, 1937, a preliminary contract recognized the CIO's Steel Workers Organizing Committee (S.W.O.C.) as bargaining agent for its members in the Carnegie-Illinois subsidiary of United States Steel. Shortly, all the steel corporation's steel-producing units entered agreements with the union. Myron Taylor had surrendered the key to Judge Gary's strategy: an absolute refusal to deal with trade unions. Why had Taylor turned from the unyielding course of his predecessor?

In 1937, the prospect of the renewal of the steel struggle looked far grimmer than it had 18 years earlier. Judge Gary could look back on four years of immense profits in 1919. The losses incident to labor troubles could be readily borne. That was hardly true in 1937. The Depression had cut deeply into earnings: from 1931 to 1934 U. S. Steel had actually operated in the red. Labor peace became imperative, however, not so much when business was bad as when it was getting better. U. S. Steel's income before taxes had climbed to $67 million in 1936, and promised to go higher in 1937. British defense orders, just then being placed, may have depended on guarantees of uninterrupted production. Taylor was intent on protecting U. S. Steel's recovery. "The cost of a strike—to the Corporation, to the public and to the men—would have been incalculable," Taylor afterward remarked.[3]

Nor was he confident of his company's ability to hold the steelworkers. The Depression called into question the paternalistic approach to labor relations. The idea of welfare capitalism rested, above all, on the company's assumption of omnipotence: that the benevolence of U. S. Steel would always protect deserving employees. Hard times had dispelled that certainty. The giant firm could not prevent unemployment, nor even relieve the hardships of its men. The steel corporation, Taylor confessed early in the Depression, was "at the mercy of business just like any other corporation."[4] The signs of labor's disaffection multiplied. A wave of sitdown strikes, culminating at General Motors in January of 1937, revealed the intensity of the discontent. Within U. S. Steel, trouble developed in the employee representation system. Like other conservative firms, the steel corporation had hastily adopted a representation plan in 1933 to forestall the National Industrial Recovery Act. Far from placating the workers, the company unions became rallying points for independent action and pro-CIO sentiment. Judge Gary, secure in his paternalistic philosophy, had discounted the union appeal. Myron Taylor could not repeat that error in 1937.

The tougher methods of labor control simultaneously broke down. Ethnic tensions, a powerful management weapon in the great strike of 1919, had died away. Restrictive immigration law had closed off the steady flow of Eastern Europeans into the mills, and the passage of time had narrowed the gulf between immigrant and native workers. The steel companies could no longer invoke loyalty from their American employees by exploiting xenophobic prejudices. Repression likewise had lost its sting. Instead of instilling caution, as hard times usually did, the Great Depression generated a courage born of desperation. Moreover, New Deal legislation now prohibited discrimination against union members. "Many individual steelworkers have, just now, a sense of freedom that has been notably absent from the steel mills since the Homestead strike of 1892," a veteran observer reported in 1936 from Homestead, Pennsylvania.[5] Nor could U. S. Steel expect to quarantine the steelworkers, as it had in 1919. The mill towns of the Pittsburgh district became open ground for CIO organizers. Early in its drive, the S.W.O.C. held a mass meeting in Homestead. The principal speaker was Thomas Kennedy, secretary-treasurer of the United Mine Workers; he also happened to be lieutenant-governor of Pennsylvania. State troopers, hitherto the scourge of strikers, escorted Kennedy to the stage. In his speech, he promised state relief for needy families in the event of a steel strike. It was a far cry from 1919.

The steel corporation faced a formidable antagonist in John L. Lewis's Committee for Industrial Organization. The National Committee for Organizing Iron and Steel Workers had suffered from weak authority, little funds, and internal dissension. On all those counts, the CIO's Steel Workers Organizing Committee was strong. And it was endowed with superb leadership. John L. Lewis, *Fortune* magazine had noted respectfully in 1936, was "a foeman worthy of U. S. Steel."[6] His able lieutenant, Philip Murray, assumed direct charge of the steel drive. Several years before, the steel corporation's coal properties—the captive mines—had come under contract with the Mine Workers. The first-hand contact had promoted grudging respect for the tough CIO leaders. The steel industry dared not, as it had in 1919, dismiss the union offensive. When the CIO announced the organizing drive in 1936, the American Iron and Steel Institute answered the challenge with a defiant advertisement in hundreds of newspapers. The mark of respect proved well justified.

Finally, the national political situation gave management small comfort. In 1919 the steel industry had capi-
talized on the Red scare to justify its fight against unionization. Public opinion could not be similarly exploited in
1937. With labor's backing, Franklin D. Roosevelt had
just won a second term; the smashing victory signified the
temper of the country. Labor's influence became apparent
on many fronts. The La Follette Civil Liberties Committee
launched its investigation of employer practices abridging
civil liberties. Obviously sympathetic to the CIO—a working arrangement actually developed—the La Follette Committee clearly was intent on exposing U. S. Steel's use of
espionage and coercion to forestall unionization. Public
officials condoned the sitdown strikes, and interceded in
industrial disputes. Roosevelt and Michigan Governor
Frank Murphy played key parts in bringing General
Motors to terms only a week before the Taylor-Lewis pact.
The Federal Government had backed off in 1919. It was
unlikely to do so in 1937.

The calculation of forces gave Myron Taylor reason for
pause. But it did not make his decision to deal with Lewis
inescapable. The S.W.O.C.'s power remained largely po-
tential in February of 1937. The steelworkers were less
extensively organized and, so far as anyone knew, less
ready to fight than they had been in September of 1919.
Even if it did reach peak strength, the CIO union could
hardly be confident of breaking the mighty steel corporation in a strike for recognition. Three months later the
Little Steel companies, resolutely open-shop despite the
defection of U. S. Steel, inflicted a heavy defeat on the
union. But Taylor was not thinking of the outcome—win or
lose—or an industrial war. Force was becoming irrelevant
to the issue of unionization. In 1919 the steelworkers had
struck to secure the privilege of collective bargaining. That
objective could now be achieved without resort to economic force. The Wagner Act of 1935 required an em-

ployer to engage in collective bargaining with any union demonstrating the support of a majority of his men. The issue that had provoked the 1919 strike no longer had to be decided on the private battlefield of American labor relations. Uncertainty, however, still clouded public policy in February 1937. The Wagner Act was in the courts, and, if precedent prevailed, seemed sure of invalidation. The confident expectation led many employers to defy the Government. Taylor disavowed such lawlessness. Even so, the Wagner Act did not force U. S. Steel to recognize the S.W.O.C. Since the union lacked a majority, U. S. Steel had no legal obligation to deal with it. So Myron Taylor could have stayed his hand with entire propriety.

In the end, Taylor acted from choice, not sheer necessity. Lewis had reason to hail him for "the farseeing vision of industrial statesmanship."[7] Taylor was convinced, whatever the fate of the Wagner Act, that the time was ending when an employer would be free, as Judge Gary had been in 1919, to fight unionization. Indeed, he had devised his formula on union recognition back in 1934, before the passage of the Wagner Act.[8] The NRA experience, inconclusive as it was, revealed to him an irreversible shift in public policy. Taylor believed in moving with the tide of change.

His situation, no less than his outlook, encouraged Taylor's flexibility. He had entered the steel corporation in 1928 as the reformer, not the executor, of Judge Gary's policies. The business needed modernization. Labor was not among Taylor's original concerns. But when the problem did arise, he was peculiarly situated to respond in new ways. The open shop was Gary's monument, not his. But if he accepted progress, Taylor also sought to mitigate its consequences. He offered recognition to the S.W.O.C., but only as representative of its own members, not of the entire work force. U. S. Steel might thereby forestall the

[184]

pressure for exclusive representation—the Wagner Act provided for a single bargaining agent for all employees in a bargaining unit—which would vault the union to a position of real power. Taylor was compromising gracefully and calculatingly. His was a response far removed from Judge Gary's rigid opposition to reform.

One characteristic Taylor and Gary did share: both represented the financial interest in steel. Over the years, however, Judge Gary came to identify himself with the industry and fell under the influence of the practical steelmen. Taylor, on the other hand, had remained purely the financial-business expert. He would revitalize U. S. Steel and, as he had done elsewhere, depart at the end of the job. The high costs of a fight over unionization concerned him deeply. He was sensitive, too, to the public interest in the affairs of U. S. Steel. And he lacked the rooted animus of the production men against trade unionism. His decision to recognize the S.W.O.C. outraged practical steelmen such as Republic's Tom Girdler and Bethlehem's Eugene Grace. They vowed to fight on without U. S. Steel. The split between Big Steel and Little Steel in 1937 reflected the historic division between the financial and steel-making interests in the industry.

Events soon passed from the hands of individuals. The Supreme Court unexpectedly upheld the Wagner Act in April of 1937. The decision bore fruit a month later at Jones and Laughlin, where an election gave the company's two big plants to the S.W.O.C. The law fulfilled its high promise through the vigorous enforcement of the National Labor Relations Board and court decisions that closed off the loopholes one by one. Meanwhile, the steel union grew more formidable. The U. S. Steel agreement itself contributed mightily, providing the S.W.O.C. with a firm membership base and a definite place in the industry, and rallying the unorganized steelworkers to the CIO banner.

Business conditions halted the union drive during the recession of 1938. But with the outbreak of World War II, the whole economy geared for defense. Business boomed and the labor market tightened. It was time to break into Little Steel.

"I won't have a contract, verbal or written, with an irresponsible, racketeering, violent, communistic body like the CIO," Tom Girdler had protested in 1937, "and until they pass a law making me do it, I am not going to do it."[9] But the law did make him do it. In mid-1941, elections and crosschecks of union membership showed CIO majorities in the plants of Republic, Bethlehem, Inland, and Youngstown Sheet and Tube. The Little Steel companies, reconciled or not, were legally obliged to bargain with the union. Even in this extremity, management retained a certain leeway to continue the fight. The Wagner Act required an employer to bargain with a union certified as representative of his men, and to do so "in good faith," but the law could not force him to make an offer acceptable to the union. This ground—the free area of collective bargaining—might be used for a last defense against unionization. Thus, months of arduous bargaining between the S.W.O.C. and Little Steel produced no agreement.

Before the stalemate could force a strike, war intervened. The Federal Government, using its emergency war powers, moved into the collective-bargaining sphere to ensure uninterrupted production. The National War Labor Board decided the unresolved issues between Little Steel and the S.W.O.C. With this award as a basis, union contracts were finally signed by the four independents in August 1942. The next month, U. S. Steel lost the advantage gained in Myron Taylor's agreement with John L. Lewis five years before. Having won a series of N.L.R.B. elections, the S.W.O.C. became the *exclusive*

bargaining agent in steel corporation plants. The War
Labor Board, finally, imposed on the protesting steel companies maintenance-of-membership (compulsory membership during the life of a contract for employees belonging
to the union at the start of the contract), a long first step
toward the union shop. So in wartime the steel industry
passed through the final stages of unionization. The CIO
had retrieved the defeat of 1919.

Was that great strike in steel thereby reduced to an
historical detail, arresting as drama, but inconsequential
in the perspective of subsequent events? It does not seem
so. The crisis of 1919 contributed its share to the later
unionization of steel. The right to organize and to engage
in collective bargaining had already grown into public
questions in 1919. The great strike dramatized the issues
and, by its effect on the President's Industrial Conference, forwarded the slow progress toward the Wagner
Act. Labor leaders themselves came away convinced that
mass-production unionism required Government intervention. Abandoning a position long held, they would
forcefully demand Federal legislation when the occasion arose in the 1930's. The passage of the Wagner Act
would, in turn, help trigger John L. Lewis' drastic decision
to launch the CIO.

The influence of 1919 extended to other fronts. The
suppression of civil liberties during the steel strike, fully
documented in the Interchurch investigation, helped to
launch the La Follette Senate Committee that effectively
exposed the repressive tactics of antiunion employers during the 1930's. The Steel Workers Organizing Committee
derived much of its effectiveness from a deliberate study
of the mistakes of 1919. "This attempt to work through a
joint committee of interested unions failed because of
the weaknesses inherent in such a set-up," concluded a
CIO memorandum. The S.W.O.C. had to operate on an

industrial-union basis. "That was the main purpose and basic difference between the two steel campaigns," CIO Director John Brophy afterward noted. "We'd learned something from the past experiences in 1918 and '19 in steel."[10] Steelmen, no less than unionists, remembered the great struggle. If steelworkers could rise once, they could again. Repetition of 1919 had to be admitted as a possibility, and its impact respected. Thus, even failure had its uses for later success.

A larger meaning also emerges. The steel strike climaxed a stage in American labor history. From that defeat there could be no appeal: mass-production unionism had to await a reordering of the established framework of American labor relations. The transformation occurred in the 1930's. The union movement abruptly changed course. Industrial unionism overcame the older pattern of trade jurisdiction. Labor's unity ended, cherished notions of internal order foundered, and the business-unionism ideology broadened. The labor movement would never be the same again. Even more notable was the expansion of public control over labor relations. In the past, unionization, no less than the terms of employment, had fallen within the private sphere. The Wagner Act placed the rights of organization and collective bargaining under public regulation. The area of voluntarism was thereby permanently contracted. And the assumption was forever abandoned that direct accommodation between labor and management could build a viable and just labor system.

So the great steel strike exacted its price from the future. American labor relations would have to be jarred from their settled framework. The upheaval occurred in the 1930's; the consequences continue to unfold.

Bibliographical Afterword

THE HISTORIAN who returns to past work after a lapse of years—more than twenty in this case—does so somewhat at his peril. Not only does he come very largely as a stranger to his own handiwork, never sure as he turns the pages whether he will be pleased or chagrined by what he encounters. He must also contend with the fact that his book has itself become an artifact of history, or rather of historiography—an expression of the particular intellectual milieu of the time in which it was written and limited by the scholarly resources then available.

Labor in Crisis stemmed from an earlier, more ambitious study, *Steelworkers in America: The Nonunion Era* (Harvard, 1960; Harper Torchbook reprint, 1969), which was an attempt to write a comprehensive history of workers in a single industry. That earlier book has been considered—rightly, I think—a transitional work between the "old" and the "new" labor history. It was intended, quite deliberately, as a departure from the institutional/trade-union approach to labor history that had prevailed ever since the days of John R. Commons.[1] *Labor in Crisis* drew heavily on *Steelworkers in America.* Chapter 1, although it contained fresh archival materials, essentially summarized the first two-thirds of *Steelworkers.* The bulk of *Labor in Crisis* relied much more on new archival research—one of the reasons, as I said in the Preface, why I was inclined to do the second book—but also recycled earlier research and drew substantially on the findings of *Steelworkers in America.* My focus had shifted, however. I was now concerned with questions of power, with labor's struggle for a voice in the industry, and with the climactic steel strike of 1919 that settled the issue for nearly twenty years. And my analysis was informed by a perspective that looked back at 1919 from the vantage point of triumphant industrial unionism during the New Deal.

Anyone who glances over the bibliography of *Steelworkers in America* will be struck by how little there is by way of contemporary scholarship—a handful of dissertations; not a single modern scholarly article; a few books of tangential importance, such as Theodore Draper's *Roots of American Communism* (New York, 1957) and Philip Taft's *The AFL in the Time of Gompers* (New York, 1957); and Robert K. Murray's *Red Scare* (Minneapolis, 1955), which contained a narrative chapter on the 1919 steel strike. In the intervening five years before *Labor in Crisis* was published, not much had changed. The only important contributions were John A. Garraty's biography, *Right-Hand Man: George W. Perkins* (New York, 1960), about a Morgan associate deeply involved in the formulation of U. S. Steel's labor policy, and his article, "The United States Steel Corporation Versus Labor: The Early Years" (*Labor History* 1 [Winter 1960]: 3–38).[2] There was not by any means a dearth of information about the steelworkers and their industry. I felt, on the contrary, singularly blessed by the richness of the primary sources, much of which stemmed from an intense interest in this pre-eminent corporate industry among progressive reformers prior to World War I. But the subject was a scholarly desert at the time I began poking around in it; I was very much on my own.

How the desert has blossomed since then! The two most important strikes before the World War have been treated in detail by John N. Ingham, "A Strike in the Progressive Era: McKees Rocks, 1909" (*Pennsylvania Magazine of History and Biography* 89 [July 1966]: 353–77) and Robert Hessen, "The Bethlehem Steel Strike of 1910" (*Labor History* 15 [Winter 1974]: 3–18). The campaign against the long workday is covered in Charles Hill, "Fighting the Twelve-Hour Day in the American Steel Industry" (*Labor History* 15 [Winter 1974]: 19–35); and the Harding administration's decisive intervention in Robert K. Murray, *The Harding Era* (Minneapolis, 1969) and Robert H. Zieger, *Republicans and Labor, 1919–1929* (Lexington, Kentucky, 1969). The Pittsburgh Survey, invaluable for understanding conditions in the steel industry, had, so far as I know, been forgotten when I first encountered it gathering dust on the shelves of the Harvard College Library. It now rates a study in its own right in John T. McClymer, "The Pittsburgh Survey, 1907–1914: Forging an Ideology in the Steel District" (*Pennsylvania History* 41 [April 1974]: 169–86), and Clarke A. Chambers has written a biography of its director, *Paul U. Kellog and the Survey: Voices for Social Welfare and Social Justice* (Minneapolis, 1971).

The industry has in recent years received considerable scholarly attention. In addition to Peter Temin's fine *Iron and Steel in Nineteenth-Century America* (Cambridge, Massachusetts, 1964), there are two broader histories: William T. Hogan, *Economic History of the Iron and Steel Industry in the U. S.* 5 vols. (Lexington, Massachusetts, 1971) and Kenneth Warren, *The American Steel Industry, 1850–1970* (London, 1973). Carnegie has been the subject of three books: Joseph Frazier Wall's definitive *Andrew Carnegie* (New York, 1970); a briefer interpretive treatment by Harold C. Livesay, *Andrew Carnegie and the Rise of Big Business* (Boston, 1975); and Louis M. Hacker, *The World of Andrew Carnegie* (Philadelphia, 1968). The most successful of Carnegie's "boys" is the subject of a solid biography by Robert Hessen, *Steel Titan: The Life of Charles M. Schwab* (New York, 1975). Hessen identifies himself as a disciple of Ayn Rand. In a curious way, his very enthusiasm for Schwab's entrepreneurial exploits—"He was the one indispensible man at Bethlehem . . . the *Arbeitgeber*—the work-giver, the man who created jobs" (198)—enabled Hessen to capture the hard-fisted reality masked by the genial Schwab's public pronouncements on labor. The closest the industry ever came to producing a genuine labor reformer was William B. Dickson, another of Carnegie's boys, a vice president of U. S. Steel and then of Midvale Steel and Ordnance. The surprising availability of Dickson's quite rich personal papers enabled Gerald G. Eggert to write a detailed account of his largely frustrated efforts, *Steelmasters and Labor Reform, 1886–1923* (Pittsburgh, 1981).

Although Frederick W. Taylor carried on his seminal experiments at Midvale Steel, scientific management did not have very much direct impact on the continuous-process steel industry. A deflating case study of Taylor's efforts— and the source of one of the choice bits of his manufactured mythology concerning Schmidt the pig-iron shoveler—is Daniel Nelson, "Taylorism and the Workers at Bethlehem Steel, 1898–1901" (*Pennsylvania Magazine of History and Biography* 101 [October 1977]: 487–505). Much more consequential was the transformation of work described in Katherine Stone, "The Origin of Job Structures in the Steel Industry" (*Radical America* 7 [November-December 1973]: 19–64 [an expanded version appeared in *Review of Radical Political Economics* 7 (Summer 1974): 61–97]). Despite a shaky command of her subject, Stone managed to delineate the fundamental shift from an earlier decentralized, casual labor system to the internal labor markets of twentieth-century steel firms. Her pioneering essay has been highly influential.

[192]

World War I briefly challenged the industry's control over its labor system. The context for that event has received a fine modern treatment in David M. Kennedy's *Over Here: The First World War and American Society* (New York, 1980). Kennedy's assessment of the war's impact on labor, however, needs to be amended by Melvyn Dubofsky's penetrating "Abortive Reform: The Wilson Administration and Organized Labor, 1913–1920" in James E. Cronin and Carmen Siriani, eds., *Work, Community and Power* (Philadelphia, 1983), 197–220. There are now, in addition, excellent monographs on the two principal wartime agencies that dealt with steel: Robert Cuff, *The War Industries Board: Business-Government Relations during World War I* (Baltimore, 1973), and Valerie Connor, *The National War Labor Board* (Chapel Hill, 1983). And the industry's relations with Washington have been usefully explored in Melvin I. Urofsky, *Big Steel and the Wilson Administration* (Columbus, Ohio, 1969). Finally, there is a thoughtful appraisal of Wilson's abortive effort at resolving the postwar labor crisis in Haggai Hurvitz, "Ideology and Industrial Conflict: President Wilson's First Industrial Conference" (*Labor History* 18 [Fall 1977]: 509–24), although the article has little to say about the politics of the conference and nothing about its relation to the 1919 steel strike.

The labor history of the evolving industry has been actively studied in the past twenty years. We have, in particular, a much better grasp of the craft era. The chapter "The Craftsmen's Empire" in Francis G. Couvares, *The Remaking of Pittsburgh: Class and Culture in an Industrializing City, 1877–1919* (Albany, New York, 1984), summarizes very effectively the current state of scholarship. Much more detailed as a case study is John W. Bennett, "Iron Workers in Woods Run and Johnstown: The Union Era, 1865–1895" (Ph.D. thesis, University of Pittsburgh, 1977). Leon Wolff, *Lockout: The Story of the Homestead Strike of*

1892 (New York, 1965), is a good narrative account; and the republican thinking of the strikers has been analyzed by Linda Schneider, "The Citizen Striker: Workers' Ideology in the Homestead Strike of 1892" (*Labor History* 23 [Winter 1982]: 47–66). Some new light on the voting behavior of Pennsylvania steelworkers, including a propensity to vote for third parties in times of industrial crisis, is shed in Michael Nash, *Conflict and Accommodation: Coal Miners, Steel Workers, and Socialism, 1890–1920* (Westport, Connecticut, 1982).

An arresting piece of comparative analysis is James Holt, "Trade Unionism in the British and U. S. Steel Industries, 1880–1914: A Comparative Study" (*Labor History* 18 [Winter 1977]: 5–35), which concludes that it was "the behavior of employers rather than employees" (34–35) that best explains the failure of trade unions in the American, as compared to the British, industry. Even more notable a comparative study is Peter R. Shergold, *Working-Class Life: The "American Standard" in Comparative Perspective, 1899–1913* (Pittsburgh, 1982), which deals with workers in Pittsburgh and Birmingham, England. Shergold's book contains the most precise and comprehensive treatment of the material conditions of life we presently have for an American working-class population. The presumed superiority of the American standard, Shergold finds, applied only to skilled workers: "The unskilled Pittsburgh worker gained a real wage that was the same as, or very little better than, that paid to the laborer in Birmingham or Sheffield" (224). Shergold draws this suggestive conclusion: that the distinguishing feature of the early twentieth-century American working class was a wage differential that made for a labor aristocracy and for a form of trade unionism—iron and steel included—reflective of its privileged status.

It is no accident that the foregoing paragraphs cite mainly local studies. The wide-ranging, opportunistic research that went into my early work on the social history of American steelworkers has given way to the deep exploration of specific steel communities. This has enabled historians to penetrate hitherto inaccessible dimensions of working-class life. In *Eight Hours for What We Will: Workers and Leisure in an Industrial City, 1870–1920* (New York, 1983), Roy Rosenzweig describes how workers spent their spare time in Worcester, Massachusetts, where the largest industrial employer after the turn of the century was U. S. Steel's American Steel and Wire Company. And Francis Couvares's *The Remaking of Pittsburgh*, previously cited, identifies a "plebeian culture" rooted in Pittsburgh's vigorous craft workers' community. According to both authors, this distinctive workers' culture was undermined first by the increasing power of industrial capital and ultimately by the emerging commercial culture of twentieth-century America. The history of working-class housewives, likewise an unexplored subject, has been opened up by Susan J. Kleinberg, "Technology and Women's Work: The Lives of Working-Class Women in Pittsburgh, 1870–1900" (*Labor History* 17 [Winter 1976]: 58–72). They were burdened especially, Kleinberg argues, by the unequal distribution of public services and by the limited access to modern household technology by wage-earning families.

Local history has also enabled scholars to penetrate more deeply into the experiences of immigrant steelworkers. In *Immigration and Industrialization: Ethnicity in an American Mill Town, 1870–1940* (Pittsburgh, 1977), John Bodnar demonstrated how heavily Slavic steelworkers in Steelton, Pennsylvania, relied on family and ethnic ties in coping with the rigors of the American industrial order as it was experienced both at the workplace and in the larger community. A more complex portrait, derived largely from intensive field research and informed by sociological theory, is Ewa Morawska, *For Bread with Butter: Life-Worlds of*

East Central Europeans in Johnstown, Pennsylvania, 1890–1940 (New York, 1985). Especially by the use of oral history, ethnic studies are adding steadily to our fund of knowledge about immigrant groups in the steel towns—e.g., Richard S. Sorrell, "Life, Work, and Acculturation Patterns of Eastern European Immigrants in Lackawanna, N.Y.: 1900–1922" (*The Polish Review* 14 [Autumn 1969]: 65–91) and M. Mark Stolarik, *Growing Up on the South Side: Three Generations of Slovaks in Bethlehem, Pennsylvania, 1880–1976* (Lewisburg, Pennsylvania, 1985).

Among ethnic historians, Bodnar has been exceptional for the attention he has paid to black workers. The findings of his Steelton research are conveniently gathered in an article, "The Impact of the 'New Immigration' on the Black Worker: Steelton, Pennsylvania, 1880–1920" (*Labor History* 17 [Spring 1976]: 214–29). In a more ambitious collaborative work that relied heavily on oral history, *Lives of Their Own: Blacks, Italians, and Poles in Pittsburgh, 1900–1960* (Urbana, Illinois, 1982), Bodnar, Roger Simon, and Michael P. Weber took issue with the school of thought that stresses the uniformities in the migratory experience of rural peoples into America's industrial centers. By considering the complex interaction of cultural traditions, family structures, race prejudice, economic opportunity, and urban processes, the authors sought to explain why blacks failed to attain the occupational and community stability achieved by the immigrant groups. On the other hand, similarities emerge from Peter Gottlieb's "Migration and Jobs: The New Black Workers in Pittsburgh, 1916–1930" (*Western Pennsylvania Historical Magazine* 61 [January 1978]: 1–15), which finds that, as with the European immigrants, the great black migration was rooted in earlier patterns of seasonal migration and that urban-rural links persisted. We have sorely lacked a comprehensive, well-grounded history of the black steelworkers. The recent publication of Dennis C. Dickerson's impressively researched *Out of the Crucible: Black Steelworkers in Western Pennsylvania, 1875–1980* (Albany, 1986) goes a long way toward meeting that need.

On the relationship of ethnicity to labor militancy, the most substantial contribution is Frank H. Serene's unpublished dissertation, "Immigrant Steelworkers in the Monongahela Valley: Their Communities and the Development of a Labor Class Consciousness" (Pittsburgh, 1979), which disputes my explanation for immigrant participation in the steel strike of 1919. It was not the wartime rupture of established patterns but a rising "labor class consciousness" that accounted for the immigrants' militancy in 1919. Church censuses suggested to Serene that immigration populations had less turnover than hitherto thought; and a study of neighborhood composition, that the various ethnic groups had substantial social contact. More problematic is the construct of class consciousness that Serene proceeds to build on the basis of these empirical findings. Industrial conflict has not figured largely in the accounts of other ethnic historians, either because the localities they chose to study lacked such conflict or because their focus on migratory patterns and community development led them away from labor issues. They have, on the whole, been inclined to stress what John Bodnar has called the "realism" of the immigrant steelworkers. Bodnar spelled out the implications of that view in "Immigration, Kinship, and the Rise of Working-Class Realism in Industrial America" (*Journal of Social History* 14 [Fall 1980]: 45–66). The encounter with industrialism, Bodnar argues, "actually fostered the growth of a family economy which sensibly sought basic economic benefits and muted individual inclinations and idealism in favor of group survival" (57). Focusing on the 1930's, Bodnar concludes that limited expectations, "the scope of family priorities," and "the desire for job security"

(58) kept the immigrant workers off the picket lines in the battle for industrial unionism. The difficulty is that they had been on the picket lines in most steel towns (although not in Bodnar's Steelton) in 1919.

That great event has itself evoked relatively little new work. Much of the scholarship already cited has added some fresh details, of course, and a handful of limited studies on the strike have appeared: Raymond A. Mohl, "The Great Steel Strike of 1919 in Gary, Indiana: Working-Class Radicalism or Trade-Union Militancy?" (*Mid-America* 63 [January 1981]: 36–52); Robert Asher, "Painful Memories: The Historical Consciousness of Steelworkers and the Steel Strike of 1919" (*Pennsylvania History* 45 [January 1978]: 61–86; Carl Meyerhuber, "Black Valley: Pennsylvania's Allekiski and the Great Steel Strike of 1919" (*Western Pennsylvania Historical Magazine* 62 [July 1979]: 251–65). But if *Labor in Crisis* perhaps still discourages further scholarship on the 1919 strike, just the opposite is true for the larger context within which that event occurred. For the history of the steelworkers in its many dimensions, my early work was merely a starting point for a rich and growing scholarship.

Labor in Crisis was conceived as a kind of prologue to the industrial-union triumph in steel of the 1930's. At the time, it seemed to me certain that the labor history of the New Deal era was about to be written. In general, that has proved true. But not for the steelworkers. Of all the great battles fought for industrial unionism, theirs is the one whose history yet remains to be told.[3]

Notes

Chapter 1

1. Quoted, David Brody, *Steelworkers in America: The Non-union Era* (Cambridge, Massachusetts, 1960), 2, 12.

2. *Ibid.*, 2, 6; U. S. House, Committee on the Investigation of the United States Steel Corporation, *Hearings*, 62 Cong., 2nd sess. (1911–12), VII, 5115.

3. Quoted, Brody, 34.

4. Quoted, Jesse S. Robinson, *The Amalgamated Association of Iron, Steel and Tin Workers* (Baltimore, 1920), 126.

5. Quoted, Brody, 53, 54; George Harvey, *Henry Clay Frick: The Man* (New York, 1928), 188.

6. Quoted, Raymond P. Kent, "The Development of Industrial Unionism in the American Iron and Steel Industry," unpublished Ph.D. thesis, University of Pittsburgh (1938), 13.

7. Minutes, Directors' Meeting, National Tube Company, Jan. 15, 1901, *United States* v. *United States Steel Corporation*, 223 F. 55 (1912), *Government Exhibits*, II, 409.

8. Arundel Cotter, *United States Steel: A Corporation with a Soul* (New York, 1921), 95; Lincoln Steffens, *The Autobiography of Lincoln Steffens* (New York, 1931), 694; American Iron and Steel Institute, *Yearbook* (1914), 284; *Fortune*, XIII (June 1936), 113.

9. George W. Perkins, memorandum, to W. E. Corey, Oct. 4, Dec. 16, 1909, Perkins to J. P. Morgan, June 25, 1906, George W. Perkins Papers, Columbia University Library.

10. Perkins to Morgan, May 22, 1908, Perkins Papers; Gary Address, Oct. 15, 1909, *U. S.* v. *U. S. Steel, Defendants' Exhibit*, II, 354.

11. *Ibid.*, 355; *U. S.* v. *U. S. Steel*, XIV, 5494; *Iron Age*, Sept. 8, 1910, 520.

12. J. P. Morgan, Jr., to Perkins, Jan. 13, 1903, Andrew Carnegie to Perkins, July 7, 1908, Perkins to E. H. Gary, Jan. 18, 1915, Perkins Papers. From George F. Baer of the Reading Coal Company, forever fixed in history as the villain in the great anthracite strike of 1902, came this sad note: "I am always interested in such plans, and all the more because my own experiments have been utter failures." Baer to Perkins, Jan. 2, 1903, Perkins Papers.

13. Perkins, memorandum, Feb. 14, 1914, Perkins Papers.

14. E. H. Gary to J. P. Morgan, April 27, 1909, Perkins to Morgan, March 11, April 12, 17, 19, 1909, Perkins Papers.

15. Perkins to Cyrus H. McCormick, July 21, 1908, Perkins Papers.

16. Perkins to J. P. Morgan, June 2, 1902, and subsequent correspondence with Morgan and Mark Hanna, Perkins Papers.

17. Quoted, Philip Taft, *The A. F. of L. in the Time of Gompers* (New York, 1957), 227.

18. Gary Address, May 29, 1911, *Addresses and Statements by Elbert H. Gary* (compiled by the Business History Society, November 1927); Brody, 175.

19. Ida Tarbell, *Elbert H. Gary* (New York, 1925), 160; Perkins to J. P. Morgan, July 27, 1907, Perkins Papers.

20. Quoted, Brody, 176.

21. Samuel Gompers to P. J. McArdle, Jan. 15, 1910, Gompers Papers, AFL-CIO Headquarters, Washington, D. C.

22. See *American Federationist,* Oct. 1901, 415–31.

23. *National Labor Tribune,* July 15, 1909; Gompers to McArdle, Dec. 18, 1909, Gompers Papers; Brody, 129.

24. AFL, *Proceedings* (1901), 240.

25. *Amalgamated Journal,* Oct. 7, 1909, 1, Dec. 7, 1911, 1; Chicago *Daily Socialist,* Oct. 13, 1909, 1; Bernard Mandel, *Samuel Gompers* (Yellow Springs, Ohio, 1964), 140.

26. AFL, *Proceedings* (1909), 226–27, 253; Gompers to George Perkins, Feb. 25, 1910, Gompers Papers.

27. Gompers to Lew Morton, Jan. 19, 1910, Gompers Papers.

28. *Amalgamated Journal,* Oct. 3, 1912, 13.

29. U. S. Bureau of Labor, *Report on Conditions of Employment in the Iron and Steel Industry* (4 vols., Washington, 1911–13), III, 139, 146; R. D. Wilson to Woodrow Wilson, June 26, 1913, R. B. Brown to W. B. Wilson, May 20, 1917, Labor Dept. Files, National Archives; "Statement of Chairman of Bethlehem Machinists before WLB Examiners," June 18, 1918, Bethlehem Case, Docket 22, National War Labor Board Files, National Archives; John Fitch, *The Steel Workers* (New York, 1911), 214, 219.

30. U. S. Bureau of Labor, *Report on Steel,* III, 507, 509.

31. R. D. Wilson to Woodrow Wilson, June 26, 1913, Labor Dept. Files; Memorandum on Proposed Profit Sharing Plan, Nov. 22, 1902, Perkins Papers.

32. Minutes, U. S. Steel Corp. Safety Committee, April 11, 1910, enclosed in R. C. Bolling to G. W. Perkins, April 11, 1910, Perkins Papers; Brody, 90.

33. Markiewicz Series, June 12, 1914, W. I. Thomas and F. Znaniecki, *The Polish Peasant in Europe and America* (2 vols., New York, 1927), I, 485; also, Brody, ch. 5, *passim*.

34. Quoted, Brody, 136, 140, 144; *American Federationist*, Sept. 1912, 718.

35. *Amalgamated Journal*, July 4, 1912, 2; Personal Interviews with Steel Workers during the summer of 1920, D. J. Saposs Papers, Wisconsin State Historical Society; AFL, *Proceedings* (1914), 385.

Chapter 2

1. *Amalgamated Journal*, Nov. 20, 1919, 10; William Z. Foster, *The Great Steel Strike and Its Lessons* (New York, 1920), 16.

2. *Iron Age*, Sept. 23, 1915, 710, Oct. 26, 1916, 948–49.

3. Quoted, Brody, *Steelworkers*, 266.

4. U. S. Senate, Special Committee Investigating the Munitions Industry, *Minutes of the War Industries Board*, 74 Cong., 1st. sess. (1935), 459–61.

5. *Iron Age*, May 4, 1916, 1082.

6. *Times* quoted, *Survey*, May 13, 1916, 190; *Minutes of War Industries Board*, 461; *Iron Age*, Aug. 16, 1917, 373; *Amalgamated Journal*, April 12, 1917, 1; *Gary Works Circle*, Feb. 1918, 7.

7. *Amalgamated Journal*, Aug. 9, 1917, 4; Amalgamated Association of Iron, Steel and Tin Workers, *Proceedings* (1918), 12774.

8. *American Federationist*, Jan. 1917, 46.

9. Woodrow Wilson to Gompers, Aug. 31, 1917, *Woodrow Wilson, Life and Letters*, ed. R. S. Baker (New York, 1939), VII, 248; W. B. Wilson to Gompers, June 6, 1917, Labor Dept. Files; Gompers to Felix Frankfurter, July 8, 16, 1918, Gompers Papers; *Survey*, Feb. 23, 1918, 575–76.

10. "Meeting of Steel Manufacturers, Waldorf-Astoria, New York City, Aug. 12, 1918," *Addresses and Statements by Gary*; Brody, 208, 211.

11. *American Federationist*, Jan. 1918, 58.

12. Hearing, June 1, 1918, Bethlehem, Penna. (typewritten); Memorandum of examiners, n.d. (June 1918); "Investigation of the Bethlehem Steel Company Controversy," June 18, 1918, 8–9, 23–24, and *passim*, Bethlehem Case, Docket 22, National War Labor Board Files, National Archives.

13. F. P. Walsh and F. M. Judson to E. G. Grace, Sept. 11, 1918, Grace to N.W.L.B., Sept 17, 1918; Minutes, executive session,

N.W.L.B., Sept. 15, 1918; Memorandum on Bethlehem case, n.d. (Sept. 1918), Docket 22, N.W.L.B. Files.

14. *Iron Age*, Aug. 8, 1918, 326, Sept. 15, 1918, 585; W. H. Taft, "What Labor Board Did and Did Not Do At Bethlehem," typewritten memorandum, n.d., Docket 22, N.W.L.B. Files; Walter Drew, Steel Fabricators of the United States, to N.W.L.B., Aug. 13, 1918, War Labor Policies Board Files, National Archives.

15. Minutes of Conference between Felix Frankfurter and E. H. Gary, *et al.*, Sept. 20, 1918, W.L.P.B. Files; I. A. Rice to W. J. Lauck, Aug. 12, Oct. 12, 1918, Report of M. S. Richmond, Oct. 8, 1918, American Sheet and Tin Plate Co. Case, Docket 232, N.W.L.B. Files.

16. "Meeting of Steel Manufacturers, Aug. 28, 1918," *Addresses and Statements by Gary;* Frankfurter to Gary, July 10, 25, Sept. 17, 19, 20, 1918, Gary to Frankfurter, July 19, 1918, Frankfurter to W. H. Taft, Oct. 18, 1918; Minutes of Conference between Frankfurter and Gary, Sept. 20, 1918, W.L.P.B. Files.

17. Quoted, Brody, 212.

18. *Amalgamated Journal*, July 11, 1918, 4; Foster, 17.

19. Interchurch World Movement, Commission of Inquiry, *Report on the Steel Strike of 1919* (New York, 1920), 147, 165.

20. W. Z. Foster to Frank P. Walsh, July 6, 1918, Walsh Papers, New York Public Library.

21. Minutes, National Committee for Organizing Iron and Steel Workers, Aug. 1–2, 1918.

22. Foster, 20.

23. Amalgamated Association, *Proceedings* (1918), 12578.

24. U. S. Senate, Committee on Labor and Education, *Investigation of Strike in the Steel Industry*, 66 Cong., 1st sess. (1919), 382.

25. *Ibid.*, 70; National Committee Release, Jan. 20, 1919; Amalgamated Association, *Proceedings* (1918), 12868.

26. Foster, 34–36; Interchurch World Movement, *Report on Steel Strike*, 169; John Brophy Memoir, Columbia Oral History Collection, 400.

27. Minutes, National Committee, Sept. 11, 1918, in D. J. Saposs, "Organizing the Steel Workers," 6, Saposs Papers, Wisconsin State Historical Society.

28. Minutes, National Committee, Aug. 1–2, 1918.

29. Fitzpatrick to Frank Walsh, Sept. 3, 1918, E. H. Nockels to Frank Morrison, Sept. 19, 1918, Walsh Papers; *Amalgamated*

Journal, Oct. 24, 1918, 28; Minutes, National Committee, Sept. 28, 1918, in Saposs, "Organizing the Steel Workers," 18.

30. *National Labor Tribune,* Dec. 12, 1918.

31. Russell (?) to W. J. Lauck, Oct. 16, 1918, Bethlehem Case, Docket 22, N.W.L.B. Files.

32. *Iron Age,* Sept. 6, 1917, 545.

33. *Gary Works Circle,* April 1917, 1.

34. J. C. Curran Address, Oct. 18, 1918, Box 13, American Steel and Wire Company Papers, Harvard Business School Library; Brody, 190–91.

35. *Activities of the Committee on Public Information* (Jan. 27, 1918), 4; Homestead *Messenger,* June 6, 1918.

36. *United Mine Workers' Journal,* March 17, 1918, cover; Brody, 222, 223; Elwood, Indiana, employees to N.W.L.B., Oct. (?) 1918, American Sheet and Tin Plate Co. Case, Docket 232, N.W.L.B. Files.

37. Brody, 229; newspaper clipping (ca. Oct. 1918), American Sheet and Tin Plate Co. Case, Docket 232, N.W.L.B. Files; Arthur Dudley to W. B. Wilson, April 23, 1918, also, W. Z. Foster to W. J. Lauck, Oct. 16, 30, 1918, Labor Dept. Files.

38. Foster, 200–201; Brody, 223.

39. *Amalgamated Journal,* Dec. 5, 1918, 17; Minutes, National Committee, Sept. 26, 1918, Jan. 4, Feb. 15, 1919, Saposs, "Organizing the Steel Workers," 9, 12.

40. E. B. Woods, "Memorandum on Bethlehem Situation," Nov. 17, 1918; E. B. Woods, report, Nov. 19, Dec. 21, 1918; R. B. Gregg to E. B. Woods, Dec. 6, 8, 9, 11, 16, 1918, Bethlehem Case, Docket 22, N.W.L.B. Files.

41. Foster, 26.

Chapter 3

1. Gary Address to U. S. Steel Subsidiary Presidents, Jan. 21, 1919, *Addresses and Statements by Gary;* Brody, *Steelworkers,* 228; F. H. Munkelt to Members, Steel Fabricators of the United States, Aug. 1, 1918, enclosing Gompers's letter, July 6, 1918, War Labor Policies Board File.

2. George W. Perkins to George W. Perkins, Jr., Nov. 3, 1918, Perkins Papers; Gary Address, Meeting of Steel Manufacturers, Dec. 9, 1918, *Addresses and Statements by Gary.*

3. Gary to Perkins, Perkins Papers, Jan. 23, 1920, Perkins Papers;

Saposs Interviews; Charles R. Walker, *Steel: The Diary of a Furnace Worker* (Boston, 1922), 77.

4. R. B. Gregg to E. B. Woods, Jan. 7, 1919, Clinton J. Koch to N.W.L.B., March 1, 1919, Bethlehem Case, Docket 22, National War Labor Board Files; Brody, 234.

5. J. S. Wisler to R. B. Gregg, Jan. 6, 1919, Bethlehem Case, Docket 22, N.W.L.B. Files; Perkins to Theodore Roosevelt, Aug. 1, 1918, Perkins Papers; Gary. Address to Subsidiary Presidents, Jan. 21, 1919, *Addresses and Statements by Gary.*

6. Quoted, Brody, 268.

7. *Iron Age,* Aug. 15, 1918, 394, March 17, 1919, 683–84.

8. *Iron Age,* Oct. 3, 1918, 810, Dec. 12, 1918, 1449; "Important Confidential Letter," Employers Association of Louisville to Members, Oct. 2, 1918, Walsh Papers; Brody, 226.

9. John D. Rockefeller, Jr., to Perkins, March 5, 1920, Perkins Papers.

10. E. G. Grace to W. H. Taft and F. P. Walsh, Dec. 12, 1918, J. S. Wisler to R. B. Gregg, Jan. 13, 1919, Paul D. Cravath to Taft, Feb. 5, 1919, Taft to Cravath, Feb. 15, 1919, R. B. Gregg to E. L. Mandel, March 5, 1919, David Williams to W. J. Lauck, March 3, 1919, Bethlehem Case, Docket 22, N.W.L.B. Files.

11. "Transcript of Proceedings," Nov. 2, 1918, Midvale Case, Docket 129, N.W.L.B. Files; *Steel Investigation,* 474; *Amalgamated Journal,* Sept. 18, 1919, 8; Brody, 235.

12. A. Pound and S. T. Moore, *They Told Barron* (New York, 1930), 82; Ben. M. Selekman, *Employes' Representation in Steel Works* (New York, 1924), 171.

13. Minutes, National Committee, March 6, 8, 1919, Saposs, "Organizing the Steel Workers," 21–23; Minutes, National Committee, April 5, 1919.

14. Interchurch World Movement, *Report on Steel Strike,* 218; Isaac J. Quillen, "Industrial City. A History of Gary, Indiana, to 1929," unpublished Ph.D. thesis, Yale, 1942, 334.

15. *Strike Investigation,* 166; Interchurch World Movement, *Report on Steel Strike,* 210.

16. *Strike Investigation,* 608; Minutes, National Committee, Nov. 25, 1918, Saposs, "Organizing the Steel Workers," 15.

17. *Amalgamated Journal,* April 25, 1918, 22; *Survey,* Jan. 4, 1919, 453.

18. *Amalgamated Journal,* Dec. 5, 1918, 1; Minutes, National Committee, Feb. 15, 1919, Saposs, "Organizing Steel Workers," 12.

19. Minutes, National Committee, April 5, 1919.

20. Mary F. Parton, ed., *Autobiography of Mother Jones* (Chicago, 1925), 211–12.

21. Interchurch World Movement, Commission of Inquiry, *Public Opinion and the Steel Strike* (New York, 1921), 188; Foster, 62; *Strike Investigation*, 508 (my italics); Tom Girdler, *Bootstraps* (New York, 1943), 176.

22. Quoted, Interchurch World Movement, *Report on Steel Strike*, 155.

23. *Ibid.*, 208.

24. *Amalgamated Journal*, Dec. 12, 1918, 29, Feb. 6, 1919, 30, Feb. 20, 1919, 23, March 20, 1919, 2; *Strike Investigation*, 493, 527; David Williams to E. B. Woods, May 23, 1919, and other letters, Bethlehem Case, Docket 22, N.W.L.B. File; Brody, 234–36.

25. Minutes, National Committee, April 5, 1919.

26. Minutes, Pittsburgh Conference, May 25, 1919, Saposs, "Organizing Steel Workers," 28–41.

27. Gary to Michael Tighe, May 20, 1919, Gompers to Gary, July 20, 1919, in *Strike Investigation*, 368, also 169.

28. Minutes, National Committee, July 11, July 20, 1919, Saposs, "Organizing Steel Workers," 43, 45–46; Brody, 237–38.

29. Minutes, National Committee, Aug. 20, 1919, Saposs, "Organizing Steel Workers," 50.

30. New York *Times*, Aug. 27, 1919.

31. Minutes, National Committee, July 20, 1919, Saposs, "Organizing Steel Workers," 46.

32. Minutes, AFL Executive Council, Aug. 28–30, 1919, 2, 12, 22; New York *Times*, Aug. 30, 1919.

33. J. P. Tumulty to Woodrow Wilson, Aug. 30, 1919, Tumulty Papers, Library of Congress; Forster to J. P. Tumulty (quoting Baruch), Sept. 9, 1919, Woodrow Wilson Papers, Library of Congress.

34. New York *Times*, Aug. 30, Sept. 20, 1919; Forster to Tumulty (quoting Baruch), Sept. 9, 1919, Woodrow Wilson Papers.

35. Forster to Tumulty (cipher telegram), Sept. 9, 1919, Tumulty to John Fitzpatrick, Sept. 10, 1919, Wilson Papers; communications from National Committee to Wilson and Tumulty printed in Foster, *Steel Strike*, 85–87.

36. Minutes, National Committee, Sept. 4, 1919, Saposs, "Organizing Steel Workers," 85; Taft, *A.F. of L. in Time of Gompers*,

389; New York *Times,* Sept. 15, 1919; Pittsburgh *Gazette-Times,* Sept. 15, 16, 1919.

37. Fitzpatrick to Gompers, Sept. 12, 1919, Gompers Papers; Minutes, National Committee, Sept. 17, 1919, Saposs, "Organizing Steel Workers," 55, 57–58.

38. *Ibid.,* 58; Brody, 240.

39. *Strike Investigation,* 98; Selekman, 168.

40. *Ibid.,* 180.

41. J. T. O'Brien to E. B. Woods, March 4, 1919, Midvale Case, Docket 129; R. B. Gregg to E. B. Woods, Dec. 9, 1918, Bethlehem Case, Docket 22, N.W.L.B. Files; Felix Frankfurter to H. F. Perkins, July 1, 1918, Perkins to Frankfurter, June 29, July 5, 1918, W.L.P.B. Files; Minutes, National Committee, April 5, 1919.

42. Cotter, *United States Steel,* 5, 257.

43. New York *Times,* Sept. 23, 1919; Allen M. Wakstein, "The Origins of the Open-Shop Movement, 1919–1920," *The Journal of American History,* LI (Dec. 1964), 467; Cotter, 248.

Chapter 4

1. *Amalgamated Journal,* March 11, 1920, 1; New York *Times,* Sept. 24, 1919; Minutes, National Committee, Sept. 27, 1919, Saposs, "Organizing the Steel Workers," 13–15; Brody, *Steelworkers,* 242.

2. *Iron Age,* Dec. 4, 1919, 1146–47.

3. ˙*Amalgamated Journal,* Sept. 11, 1919, 25, Sept. 25, 1919, 26, Oct. 2, 1919, 1, 18.

4. *Proceedings of the First Industrial Conference, October 6 to 23, 1919* (Washington, 1920), 114.

5. W. Z. Foster to Gompers, Oct. 7, 1919, in Minutes, AFL Executive Council, Oct. 5–22, 1919, 15; New York *Times,* Sept. 29, 1919.

6. Woodrow Wilson to Gompers, Sept. 3, 1919, in *Proceedings of Industrial Conference,* 283 (identical letter to others).

7. Bernard Baruch *et al.,* to Woodrow Wilson, Oct. 24, 1919, Labor Dept. Files; Franklin Lane to Woodrow Wilson, Oct. 19, 1919, Woodrow Wilson Papers; *Proceedings of Industrial Conference,* 58.

8. *United Mine Workers' Journal,* Oct. 1, 1919, 6; Gary to Woodrow Wilson, Oct. 16, 1919 (carbon draft of letter not sent),

Perkins Papers; Forster to J. P. Tumulty, Sept. 9, 1919, Woodrow Wilson Papers; Industrial Conference File, Labor Dept. Files.

9. Gary to Woodrow Wilson, October 16, 1919 (draft of letter not sent), Perkins Papers; Minutes, Meeting of Public Group, National Industrial Conference, Oct. 14, 15, 1919, Labor Dept. Files.

10. Gary to Woodrow Wilson, Oct. 16, 1919 (two drafts of letters not sent), Perkins Papers.

11. *Proceedings of Industrial Conference*, 220 ff.; description of session in New York *Times*, Oct. 21, 1919.

12. *Proceedings of Industrial Conference*, 141, 233, 236, 255; Minutes, Meeting of Public Group, Oct. 15, 16, 20, 21, 1919, Labor Dept. Files.

13. *Proceedings of Industrial Conference*, 175, 189.

14. Minutes, AFL Executive Council, Oct. 5–22, 1919, 75, 77–78.

15. Franklin Lane to Woodrow Wilson, Oct. 19, 1919, Wilson Papers; New York *Times*, Oct. 22, 1919; *Proceedings of Industrial Conference*, 248.

16. *Ibid.*, 250.

17. *Ibid.*, 251–52.

18. *Strike Investigation*, 162–65, 172.

19. Quoted, *Literary Digest*, Oct. 18, 1919, 12–13.

20. *Proceedings of Industrial Conference*, 274–75.

21. Frank Duffy to Gompers, Sept. 30, 1919, in Minutes, AFL Executive Council, Oct. 5–22, 1919, app.; *American Federationist*, Dec. 1919, 1125; New York *Times*, Oct. 23, 1919.

22. Bernard Baruch to Woodrow Wilson, Oct. 24, 1919, Labor Dept. Files. (My italics.)

23. New York *Times*, Sept. 24, 1919.

24. Quoted, *Literary Digest*, Oct. 4, 1919, 12, Oct. 11, 1919, 11–12.

25. Foster, *Steel Strike*, 110; Stanley Coben, *A. Mitchell Palmer: Politician* (New York, 1963), 196. On the Red scare, see Stanley Coben, "A Study of Nativism: The American Red Scare of 1919–20," *Political Science Quarterly*, LXXIX (March 1964), 52–75; Robert K. Murray, *Red Scare* (Minneapolis, Minn., 1955).

26. John B. Lennon to H. L. Kerwin, Sept. 26, 1919, Federal Mediation and Conciliation Service Files, National Archives.

27. Quoted, *Literary Digest*, Oct. 4, 1919, 10.

28. *Proceedings of Industrial Conference*, 116; J. P. Tumulty to Robert Lansing, Oct. 28, 1919, Tumulty Papers.

29. New York *Times,* Sept. 24, 1919.

30. *Strike Investigation,* 306, 481.

31. *Literary Digest,* Oct. 11, 1919, 12; New York *Times,* Sept. 24, 1919; *Gary Works Circle,* Sept. 1919; Donora, Penna., *Evening Herald,* Dec. 6, 1919; Central Tube Co. to Woodrow Wilson, Aug. 30, 1919, F.M.C.S. Files.

32. Interchurch World Movement, *Public Opinion and Steel Strike,* 125 ff.

33. New York *Times,* Sept. 24, 26, 1919.

34. Leonard Wood to George W. Perkins, Jan. 3, 1920, Perkins Papers.

35. *Strike Investigation,* 915–16, 951; Quillen, "Gary," 368; Brody, 247.

36. *Strike Investigation,* 112; Minutes, National Committee, April 5, 1919.

37. *Iron Age,* Sept. 18, 1919, 782–87, Sept. 25, 1919, 876–87.

38. Pittsburgh *Gazette-Times,* Sept. 24, 1919; William Z. Foster and E. C. Ford, *Syndicalism* (n.p., 1911) 3, 28.

39. New York *Times,* Sept. 24, 1919.

40. *Ibid.,* Sept. 25, Oct. 1, 1919.

41. *Amalgamated Journal,* Oct. 1, 1919, 2. The line of argument in this paragraph is a composite of many statements made before the Senate investigating committee and in press interviews and speeches.

42. *Strike Investigation,* 418; *Iron Age,* Sept. 18, 1919, 783.

43. *Strike Investigation,* 111, 432; Mandel, *Gompers,* 432–34; *Literary Digest,* Oct. 11, 1919, 11–13; New York *Times,* Oct. 13, 1919.

44. *Strike Investigation,* 386–87, 390, 396, and *passim.*

45. Jacob Margolis, in *Strike Investigation,* 826; Foster, 262.

46. E. T. Flood to F. P. Walsh, Oct. 9, 1918, Walsh Papers; Frank Morrison to AFL Executive Council members, Dec. 6, 7, 1920, enclosing AFL organizers' reports of Foster's speeches, Frank Duffy Papers, Harvard Labor-Management History Project; Samuel Gompers, *Seventy Years of Life and Labor* (2 vols., New York, 1925), II, 514–18.

47. Minutes, National Committee, Dec. 5, 1919; John Brophy Memoir, Columbia Oral History Collection, 406–8.

48. *Proceedings of Industrial Conference,* 214–15; New York *Times,* Oct. 1, 11, 1919; Interchurch World Movement, *Public Opinion and Steel Strike,* 335.

49. Tumulty to Robert Lansing, Oct. 28, 1919, and earlier letters to Wilson, Tumulty Papers.

50. H. L. Kerwin to J. A. Wilson, Sept. 26, 1919, to J. M. Jones, Nov. 10, 1919, A. M. Palmer to W. B Wilson, Oct. 14, 1919, and other documents, including undated memorandum, in 170–763 file, F.M.C.S. Files; Minutes, National Committee, Dec. 1, 1919; *Amalgamated Journal*, Nov. 13, 1919, 2, Dec. 4, 1919, 7.

Chapter 5

1. Raymond F. Fosdick, *John D. Rockefeller, Jr.* (New York, 1956), 174.

2. *Strike Investigation*, 548 ff., 603–604; affidavits, Interchurch World Movement, *Public Opinion and Steel Strike*, 183–85.

3. *Strike Investigation*, 998 ff.

4. *Amalgamated Journal*, Oct. 16, 1919, 4, 17; J. A. Wilson to W. B. Wilson, Sept. 24, 1919, Federal Mediation and Conciliation Service Files.

5. Interchurch World Movement, *Public Opinion and Steel Strike*, 177; *Strike Investigation*, 742–44, 754.

6. *Ibid.*, 794, 885, 886, 1000.

7. Henry Streifler to Frank Morrison, Jan. 17, 1920, Duffy Papers.

8. New York *Times*, Sept. 24, 27, 1919; Foster to Gompers, Oct. 7, 1919, in Minutes, AFL Executive Council, Oct. 5–22, 1919, 15.

9. *Ibid.*

10. *Strike Investigation*, 1000.

11. John DeYoung and Ed Nockels to A. M. Palmer, N. D. Baker, and W. B. Wilson, Oct. 10, 1919, Baker to W. B. Wilson, Oct. 12, 1919, Palmer to W. B. Wilson, Oct. 14, 1919, F.M.C.S. Files.

12. New York *Times*, Sept. 24, 30, 1919; *Iron Age*, Dec. 4, 1919, 1146–47.

13. United Mine Workers of America, *Proceedings* (1919), 509; *Amalgamated Journal*, Sept. 11, 1919, 21, Oct. 9, 1919, 1; Laughlin Lodge #87, Amalgamated Association of Iron, Steel and Tin Workers, to W. B. Wilson (undated; received Jan. 24, 1920) F.M.C.S. Files.

14. New York *Times,* Sept. 30, 1919; *Strike Investigation,* 515–16.

15. *Iron Age,* Aug. 9, 1923, 332; Interchurch World Movement, *Public Opinion and Steel Strike,* 10 and ch. 4; Saposs Interviews; Brody, *Steelworkers,* 261; Minutes, National Committee, Nov. 24, 1919, Saposs, "Organizing Steel Workers," 132.

16. Pittsburgh *Gazette-Times,* Sept. 30, 1919; Quillen, "Gary," 349, 358; Brody, 258.

17. Quillen, 358–59; *Amalgamated Journal,* Oct. 2, 1919, 4, Nov. 13, 1919, 10.

18. *Strike Investigation,* 177; Interchurch World Movement, *Public Opinion and Steel Strike,* 28–30 and ch. 1, *passim; Fortune,* XIII (May, 1936), 136.

19. Interchurch World Movement, *Public Opinion and Steel Strike,* 132–40; Foster, *Steel Strike,* 167–68.

20. *Amalgamated Journal,* Nov. 20, 1919, 16, Dec. 25, 1919, 11; Johnstown *Leader,* Nov. 18, 1919; Interchurch World Movement, *Public Opinion and Steel Strike,* 138; New York *Times,* Sept. 26, 1919.

21. Minutes, National Committee, Dec. 13–14, 1919; Brody, 254; E. R. McKinney Memoir, Columbia Oral History Collection, 26.

22. Foster, 197–98; Minutes, National Committee, Nov. 24, 1919, Saposs, "Organizing Steel Workers," 130–32.

23. *Iron Age,* Nov. 27, 1919, 1093; Donora *Evening Herald,* Dec. 6, 1919; Foster to Gompers, Nov. 8, 1919, in Minutes, AFL Executive Council, Nov. 9–12, 1919, 13.

24. *Strike Investigation,* 382; *Machinists Journal,* Feb. 1920, 131–32.

25. *Amalgamated Journal,* May 8, 1919, 2; *National Labor Tribune,* May 20, 1920; Brody, 256.

26. *Strike Investigation,* 632 ff. prints contract, also, 668.

27. Minutes, National Committee, Dec. 13–14, 1919; Tighe to William Dobson, Dec. 17, 1919, in Minutes, National Committee, June 16, 1920; *Iron Age,* Feb. 5, 1920, 415; Brody, 257; Tighe to Gompers, Feb. 23, 1920, in Minutes, AFL Executive Council, Feb. 24–March 3, 1920, 77.

28. *National Labor Tribune,* May 20, 1920.

29. *Iron Age,* Nov. 6, 1919, 13.

30. Minutes, National Committee, Dec. 1, 13–14, 1919; Interchurch World Movement, *Public Opinion and Steel Strike,* 71–74, 331–41; Foster, 156–60.

31. Minutes, National Committee, Dec. 1, 1919; Foster, 193.

32. *Machinists Journal,* April 1920, 357; L. Matt Green to W. B. Wilson, Jan. 25, 1920, F.M.C.S. Files; Saposs Interviews.

33. Brody, 277.

34. Gary Address, May 28, 1920, *Addresses and Statements by Gary; Iron Age,* June 3, 1923, 1608.

35. Correspondence with W. B. Wilson, 170–763 file, F.M.C.S. Files; Philip C. Ensley, "The Interchurch World Movement and the Great Steel Strike of 1919," unpublished M.A. thesis, Ohio State University, 1962, 73–74.

36. George W. Perkins to Gary, Jan. 22, 1920, Perkins Papers.

Chapter 6

1. Myron C. Taylor, *Ten Years of Steel* (Hoboken, New Jersey, 1938), 41–42. For a detailed description, see *Fortune,* XV (May 1937), 91 ff.

2. New York *Daily News,* March 2, 1937.

3. Taylor, 43.

4. *Fortune,* XIII (June 1936), 113.

5. Quoted, Walter Galenson, "The Unionization of the American Steel Industry," *International Review of Social History,* I (1956), 12–13.

6. *Fortune,* XIII (May 1936), 144.

7. Quoted, Galenson, 20.

8. The original formula of 1934 did lack the following italicized words: "It will negotiate *and contract* with the representatives of any group of its employees. . . ." Cf. Taylor, 34, 41–42. This was a significant concession, but one which stemmed logically from the original formula.

9. *Fortune,* XVI (Nov. 1937), 168.

10. Katherine Pollak, "Craft Failures in Steel in Earlier Campaigns," typewritten memorandum, June 15, 1936, CIO Papers, Catholic University of America; Brophy Memoir, Columbia Oral History Collection, 699.

Bibliographical Afterword

1. For an account of the writing of *Steelworkers,* see my essay "Workers and Work in America: The New Labor History" in James B. Gardner and George Rollie Adams, eds., *Ordinary Lives and Everyday People* (Nashville, Tennessee, 1983), 142–45.

2. The regrettable absence of a citation to Garraty's book in the notes I attribute to the fact that I went back for my information to the Perkins Papers on which Garraty had based his biography and which subsequently were deposited at the Columbia University Library.

3. The most recent survey of the industrial-union literature is the Bibliographical Essay in Robert H. Zieger, *American Workers, American Unions, 1920–1985* (Baltimore, 1986).

Index

[213]

Index

Index

Smart, George, 140
Solidarity, 139
South Bethlehem, Pa., 84, 109
South Chicago, Ill., 69, 97, 112
Sproul, Gov. W. C., 153
Stationary Engineers union, 65
Steel companies, Big and Little Steel, 110, 183, 185, 186; fight unionization, 7, 26, 35–36, 44, 78, 87–95, 110; at Industrial Conference, 116–28, 146, 147, 148–55, 163–64; key to widespread unionization, 8, 27–28, 45, nature of management, 13–18, 25; price fixing, 21–22; treatment of workers, 15–18, 47–48 (*See also* Welfare benefits; Employee representation); and War, 46–48, 50–62. *See also* individual companies
Steel Fabricators' Association, 56, 78
Steel Strike of 1919, 108, 111, 112–15; pressure for, 95–100, 107; National Committee and, 100–01, 105; Wilson asks postponement, 105–06; production during, 113; debated at Industrial Conference, 116–25, 128; called radical conspiracy, 128–134; leads to Red hunt, 134–36; discredited by Foster incident, 136–44; terror and repression, 148–55, 164; Government refuses to intervene, 145–46; industrial espionage during, 159–160; disintegration, 168–70; sympathy strikes, 170–71; grinds to an end, 171–75; Interchurch mediation, 172–74; evaluation of, 175–79, 187–88. *See also* Press
Steel Workers Organizing Committee, 180, 182–88
Steelton, Pa., 43
Stockyards Labor Council, 62, 66
Strikebreakers, 152, 162–63, 175
Strikes, before 1919, 17–18, 26–27, 28, 42, 43, 47, 53, 82
Supreme Court, 185
Syndicalism, 137–38

Taft, William H., 55, 60, 84
Taylor, Frederick W., 15
Taylor, Myron C., 179–85, 186
Tighe, Michael, 33, 114, 168, 169
Topping, John A., 47
Tumulty, Joe, 103–06, 122, 131, 145

Unemployment, 41, 80
Union members, discrimination against, 35–36, 52, 53, 54, 87, 88–89, 96, 97, 175, 182
Unionization, 7, 18, 25, 26, 32–33, 34–38, 42-44, 49–50; World War I opportunities, 49, 50, 53, 60–63; 1918 drive, 8, 63–76; management combats, 78–86, 87–95; second campaign dropped, 176; CIO drive, 182–184; effect of Wagner Act, 183–185; and Little Steel, 186–87
Unions, national, 7, 33, 49, 64–69, 106, 165–66; jurisdictional problems; 30–31, 32, 65, 169–70; Government attitude toward, 61; recognition of, 55, 58, 111, 115, 116; issue at Industrial Conference, 116–28 *passim*
United Mine Workers, 64, 68, 92, 93, 127, 130, 170, 182
U. S. Steel Corp., 14, 15, 19, 20–21, 22, 48, 71, 134, 186; and unions, 26–29, 30, 33, 49, 56–57, 89, 98, 99, 102, 103, 108, 110, 118, 120, 144, 147, 148, 152, 174, 179–85; treatment of workers, 22–24, 37, 39, 47, 71, 73–74, 78–79, 81, 82, 108, 114, 132, 176

Van Buren, Lieut. Donald C., 135–36
Vandergrift, Pa., 36
Voluntarism, 7, 50, 104, 188

Wage stability, 24, 79, 80
Wages, as labor-management issue, 15–17, 24, 39–40, 42, 48, 53–54, 70–71, 85, 86, 96, 98, 101, 108, 114, 130, 156, 178